SOUL OF THE SEA

IN THE AGE OF THE ALGORITHM

HOW TECH STARTUPS CAN HEAL OUR OCEANS

GREGORY S. STONE   **NISHAN DEGNARAIN**

LEETE'S ISLAND BOOKS, SEDGWICK, MAINE

Dedicated to the pioneers, innovators and crew of Spaceship Earth who are committed to improving the state of our oceans.

Contents

FOREWORD

by Ambassador Peter Thomson
President of the UN General Assembly
5 June 2017

The ocean is in deep trouble.

Destructive fishing practices are pervasive, many of them illegal and unreported; while the absurdities of fisheries subsidies play on, even as the very fish-stocks these industrialised fishing fleets pursue reach tipping points of collapse. The scale of degraded coastal ecosystems and marine pollution is out of hand. There will be more plastic in the ocean than fish by 2050. When it comes to the ocean's health, the old throw-away adage of "dilution is the solution to pollution" clearly no longer holds water. From rising water temperatures to rising acidity levels to rising sea levels, the implications for humanity are not good.

But with timely action, human-induced problems have human-produced solutions. Thus it is that the time has come for us to act, to remedy the woes we have put upon the ocean, to reverse the cycle of decline our cumulative habits have imposed upon the marine environment.

So much of our culture, leisure, and well-being derives from our joy in the beauty and bounty of the ocean. Half of the oxygen we breathe comes from it; in fact the massive daily vertical migration of life between the ocean's epipelagic and mesopelagic zones pumps the lungs of Planet Earth. Over 3 billion humans depend on marine produce for their sustenance and livelihoods. The ocean is a vast reservoir of biodiversity with around 200,000 species already identified and millions more likely to be discovered. Do we really want to give all that away? Are we really prepared to surrender to the inexorable spread of hypoxic dead zones advancing along our shores, to greedy oil slicks decimating wildlife and ecosystems, to a cascading farewell for so many species forever, to the magical myriads of colour and life-forms of the world's coral reefs turning into ashen memorials of what was once so wonderful?

Gandhi was prescient when he observed the world has enough for everyone's need, but not enough for everyone's greed. Humanity's consumption and production patterns, coupled with our exponential population growth and the impacts of climate change, have become the existential challenges of our time. Recognizing that humanity's current path is unsustainable, in 2015 world leaders unanimously adopted the Paris Climate Agreement and the 2030 Sustainable Development Agenda.

Taken together, if faithfully implemented these two universal agreements will take humanity off that path toward unsustainability.

The 2030 Sustainable Development Agenda contains 17 goals, known as the SDGs. One of these, SDG14, is the goal to conserve and sustainably use the resources of the ocean. SDG14 sets targets that address the problems we have put upon the ocean, including marine pollution, acidification, overfishing, protection of marine and coastal ecosystems, and ocean governance. We are mandated to work this goal through to success by 2030, and all those of us on this planet who care about the health of the ocean should muster our ideas and energy to support its success.

Whether your interests lie in the public or private sector, whether your country has a coastline or not, whether you eat marine produce or don't, whether you're rich or poor, young or old, the ocean's health is going to affect you and your children. You have a stake in the success or failure of SDG14. So I present a challenge to all: take on board the logic of sustainability, and going forward make the choices as individuals and as groups that support the implementation of SDG14 and the good outcomes of The Ocean Conference.

Even as we have a moral duty not to steal from our grandchildren's future, we have an existential selfish imperative to halt the degradation of the ocean's health. Take up the challenge. Here's an easy start: henceforth only eat fish from a sustainable fishery.

And on the subject of that challenge, I thank the authors of this book, Greg Stone and Nishan Degnarain, for all they are doing to meet it.

The sea is everything.

*It covers seven-tenths of the terrestrial globe.
Its breath is pure and life-giving. It is an immense
desert where man is never lonely, for he senses
the weaving of Creation on every hand. It is the
physical embodiment of a supernatural existence.
For the sea is itself nothing but love and emotion.
It is the Living Infinite, as one of your poets has
said. Nature manifests herself in it, with her three
kingdoms: mineral, vegetable, and animal.
The ocean is the vast reservoir of Nature.*

— Jules Verne (1870)
Twenty Thousand Leagues Under the Sea

Preface

OUR OCEANS are a source of wonder for many of us. They have inspired generations of artists, novelists, filmmakers, and musicians; beaches are filled with children's laughter and childhood memories; new discoveries continue to confound and astonish our scientists; religions have been shaped by them; billions depend on the oceans for trade, food, and their livelihood; and they are often a place for reflection and contemplation, where many enjoy swimming, diving, and relaxing by the sea. They are a thing of beauty.

Yet they are a system under duress. The challenges our oceans face will not solve themselves unless there is a proactive effort by all leaders. Government leaders alone will not come to the rescue. It will take a united front. There are some very strong vested interests and equally strong opinions. Leadership is a contact sport, and ocean leadership will not be painless.

The purpose of the book is not to describe the decline of the oceans but to point the direction where solutions may lie. Nor have we have set out—in the words of Enric Sala—to write the obituary of the oceans and go into excruciatingly morbid details of the nature of the thousands cuts that are bleeding them dry. This is not a book about scapegoats, 'bad guys' and who to blame for the ocean's decline. Neither is it about pointing fingers at colonial history, the greed of capitalism, or illicit trade around the world. However, in order to understand where we are going, it is important to understand where we have come from. It is about understanding that we are part of a system—a dynamic and fluid system, in constant motion.

This is a book about solutions.

We need solutions. Not just to meet an existential challenge, but solutions that could also open up exciting new frontiers in terms of low-cost clean energy, fresh water, sustainable food, and new cures for illness. The next century could be our most exciting yet, enhanced by a new machine age.

Solutions may not come from any one sector. We refer to 'tech startups' in our subtitle, but tech is not just about apps, gadgets, and widgets. It is a mindset. It is about disrupting the status quo. It is about the radically new business models that might come from startups but which can be applied more widely to addressing society's biggest challenges.

This book is also about the power of youth.

Who could have imagined that one of the most influential businesses and philanthropic organisations of all time would come from a 20-year-old university dropout? Who could have predicted that the world's most valuable company would be founded by a 22-year-old and 23-year-old working out of a garage in Menlo Park? Who could have anticipated that a company with the potential to connect billions, transform the media industry, and be responsible for the rise and fall of governments, would be the brainchild of a 20-year-old student? In a world hungry for heroes, whose stories of inspiration will bring us light amid the darkness, where will the next heroes of the ocean come from? Who will be the next Bill Gates, Larry Page, Sergey Brin, or Mark Zuckerberg of our natural world?

These leaders would be the first to tell you that today's youth has just as much to offer—maybe more.

On the eve of a major global UN conference on addressing the decline of our oceans, we're looking for bolder, smarter solutions. We're looking for ideas that overturn convention and challenge perceived wisdom. We need a new injection of energy and perspective from different corners of our complex societies. Some of these solutions may lie in the minds of our youth. Some may lie in the far-flung, often forgotten, small islands of the world. With today's technological tools, it is often just the limits of our mind's creativity and our heart's courage that are holding us back.

What if we could take all this creativity, all this energy, ingenuity, drive, and optimism, and use it to address some of the biggest challenges our planet faces?

Our power to affect the environment for better or worse has never been greater. We can use this power to reduce the decline in ocean health, restore it, and guarantee its future.

So in the end this book is also about hope. It's about who we are as individuals and as a species and how we want to be remembered. Beneath all the technology, beneath the politics and the economics, this is a book about the future—the planet's, the ocean's, our own.

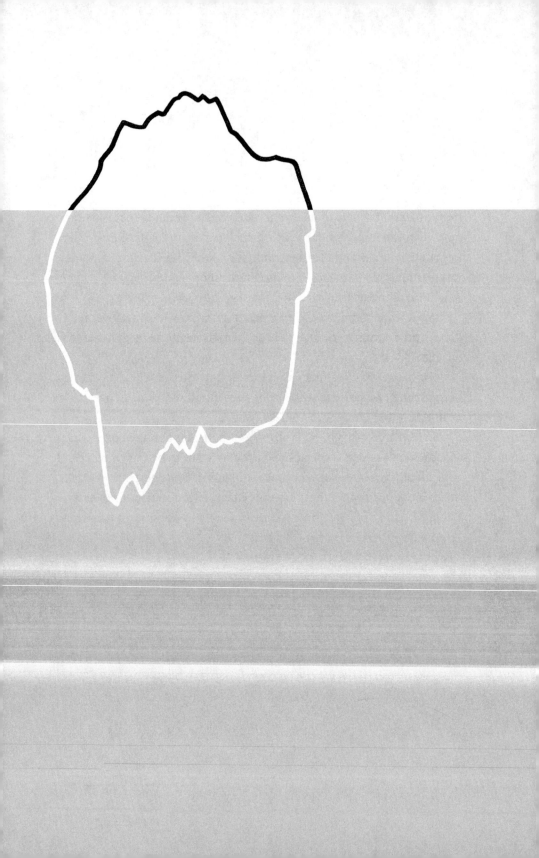

Introduction

SPACESHIP EARTH, as Buckminster Fuller noted, does not come with an operating manual.

We need to write one, and we need to do it quickly. 'We' the policy-makers and scientists, 'we' the politicians and academics, 'we' the businessmen and women; 'we' the fishermen and farmers; 'we' the consumers and 'we' the concerned citizens; 'we' the rich, 'we' the poor, and everybody in the middle; 'we' in the West and 'we' in the East, the North, and the South.

All of us.

We stand at the beginning of a new technological age, a new industrial revolution that promises radical change to the way we do business, the way we live our day-to-day lives, and the way we view our place in the world. Our power to affect the environment for better or worse has never been greater. We can choose to use this power to halt the decline in ocean health, restore it, and guarantee its future, or we can stand passively by. How we act and react in the next few years will reveal who we really are.

The battle ahead is for the soul of the sea, but it is also a battle for our own future. The decisions we take now about how we treat the ocean, will affect the quality of our existence for hundreds and perhaps thousands of years. Victory is not a foregone conclusion. We have a small window of opportunity in which to act. Our understanding of the ocean's decline is developing fast and we have the ability to address, halt, and reverse it. This window is closing—and there are no passengers on Spaceship Earth. We are all crew.

When he coined the term 'Spaceship Earth,' in 1967, Fuller could have been looking at one of the first photographs of the world taken from space. He saw a small, delicate sphere, mostly blue, apparently suspended in nothingness, apparently motionless but hurtling around the sun at 67,000 miles an hour.

There is no resupply for Spaceship Earth. All the water we will ever drink, all the food we will ever eat, all the air we will ever breathe is already on board in one form or another.

The life-support system that manages all these and the biggest driver of what happens to our climate is the ocean. There is more heat stored in the first 10 feet of the ocean than in the entire atmosphere. It drives the hydrologic cycle, harbours 80% of all living organisms, absorbs 30% of the carbon dioxide we produce, generates over 50% of the oxygen in the atmosphere, and accounts for over 95% of the habitable space on the planet. This life-support system, however, is operating at the limit of its specifications. Ocean health has been deteriorating rapidly for over a century.

If we don't do something to halt this decline and restore ocean health, life will of course go on—just maybe not in a manner, comfort level, or cost that is acceptable for humans. Humanity has learned hard lessons on land when it comes to our ability to cause extinctions. It is estimated that our presence on the planet has increased extinction rates by 100 to 1,000 times the natural rate. Science has only documented 15 marine animal species to extinction, as opposed to 514 on land. This 36-fold difference can be explained by the fact that we have been disrupting terrestrial systems for far longer. We are catching up and well into a phase of large-scale ecological disruption in the ocean and, as McCauley et al. (2015) warn, if we continue on our current path of fishing and habitat destruction, "...we may finally trigger a wave of marine extinctions of the same intensity as that observed on land."

First of all, we have to recognise the opportunity we have right now to get to work. The ocean is opaque and, as land animals, our understanding of it is limited. The surface may look blue from above, but below mayhem ensues. We have been mapping the land for millennia, yet our maps of the ocean are centuries old and still leave a great deal to be desired. Even our maps of celestial bodies like the moon and Venus are more accurate and more comprehensive than those of the sea floor. Similarly, we have been studying land-based ecologies for centuries but ocean-based ones for merely a matter of decades. Our understanding and management of the ocean is equally primitive in comparison. It was some 10,000 years ago that we first tamed nature by cultivating crops and then domesticating wild animals to feed us, but it is only very recently that we finally developed the techniques and technologies to tame the wild animals of the sea.

We are, however, currently experiencing an ocean renaissance, a rare syzygy, a precious moment of alignment. We are waking up to the ocean's importance, and it is currently at the forefront of the public consciousness and top of the global agenda. We have not seen its like for 35 years, since 1982 when, after decades of negotiation, the world came together and agreed to the United Nations Convention on the Law of the Sea (UNCLOS or Law of the Sea).

Although some countries—notably the United States—have not ratified this treaty, we are nonetheless seeing a renewed focus unlike anything we've seen in a generation. Two major UN agreements made in 2015, the Paris Agreement on Climate Change and the Sustainable Development Goals, commit the world to ocean sustainability. Despite a cluttered global agenda, the world of public policy has— finally, fortunately, and not a moment too soon—woken up to how important the ocean is.

Before we cast about for solutions we need to identify the precise causes of the problem, many of which have resulted from what we might consider our extraordinary success as a species. We're the most adaptable and intelligent animal to ever appear on Earth. 'Only a human,' Haldane noted, 'can run twenty miles, swim a mile and climb a tree.' From one corner of one continent millions of years ago we now find ourselves occupying every continent and wielding the power to transform almost everything we touch. This, of course, has enabled our numbers to flourish, gradually and then explosively. It wasn't until the start of the 19th century that the global population hit a billion. It reached 2 billion by 1927 and today, less than a century later, we're at over 7 billion and our life expectancy is rising as well. As our numbers grow, so we take more of what we need from the ocean and put back in more of that which we don't. And as more and more of us aspire to ever-greater standards of living in our carbon-based economy, our greenhouse gas emissions increase, our climate changes and the acidity of the oceans rises.

Our next challenge lies in formulating and applying effective, holistic solutions that can adapt themselves to the task as it, too, evolves. That same power we wield to exploit and modify our world can be used to solve the problems we created along the way. The solutions we're looking for are not simply an extension or fine-tuning of the traditional ideas, tools, technologies, and ways of thinking surrounding traditional resource conservation management. The very nature of the crisis facing our oceans has changed and is unprecedented in scope, scale, and urgency. Static, linear solutions for a dynamic, non-linear system will not work. It's not simply a matter of damage limitation or mitigating the human impact. Our economic systems, our governance, our environmental interventions must be rethought, reorganised, and retooled.

We need radically new ways of thinking and behaving. Our priorities must be reordered and even the very values that guide our progress must be challenged and, where necessary, refined, or replaced. We need dynamic, non-linear solutions for a dynamic, non-linear system.

We need radically new ways of cooperating, too. The innovations and developments that in the past we may have seen as unrelated must be brought together. Existing disciplines and techniques must be woven together with advances in fields such as Big Data and Artificial Intelligence, autonomous machines and low-cost sensors, nanotechnology and behavioral economics, genetics and synthetic biology.

Collectively dubbed 'the Fourth Industrial Revolution' by Klaus Schwab of the World Economic Forum, these technological, economic, and social advances are quickly and completely transforming every aspect of our society. They must now be applied to how we think about, use, and care for the oceans. Some species and ecosystems have already been lost for ever. The flightless bird, the dodo, is perhaps the most famous example, a now-proverbial symbol of man's carelessness.

Within just 64 years of the first sighting in Mauritius by the Dutch, it was consigned to history by 1662 due to a combination of greed, habitat destruction, and the unintended introduction of invasive species.

We are currently losing several species to extinction every single day at a rate that's between a hundred and a thousand times above the normal, natural one. What is perhaps less well known is that local extirpations are also a regular occurrence. In many ways, these extirpations, or local extinction events, are as serious as global extinction occurrences, with the loss of genetic material or the functioning that these species play in a local ecosystem being critical to the well-being of these environments. It is the land-based equivalent of losing a population of honeybees, and the pollination function they provide in a particular region.

In the past, we could have claimed ignorance. But we can see how our actions affect the ocean. We know about declining fish stocks and marine pollution. We know about the invasive species we have introduced to new ecosystems and the devastating effects they can have. We know about the imminent collapse of coral reefs and we know about the melting ice caps. Though we know all this, we have yet to take full responsibility and remedial action.

The challenge is three-fold. We must first stabilise the patient and stop the decline in ocean health. We must then restore conditions to a healthy state. At the same time, we must develop a new way of living, working, and thriving that ensures a harmonious and sustainable relationship with the ocean.

Ultimately, it is not the ocean's survival that's at stake. It's our own.

CHAPTER ONE

One planet, one experiment.

— Edward O. Wilson
The Diversity of Life

Our Ocean
Civilisation

Pushing the Boundary

ANY SYSTEM—biological, financial, mechanical, or digital—has safe operating limits. The trouble is that without an operating manual we don't know where precisely these limits are when it comes to Spaceship Earth. We do, however, know that we're exceeding several already.

We also know that, even within these limits or planetary boundaries, there are tipping points. Past these points, things begin to go swiftly, irreversibly, unpredictably, dangerously, and even fatally wrong. Our momentum can then carry us clean through the boundaries and leave us stranded on the other side.

These boundaries and tipping points apply wherever we look to our global commons, a phrase used to refer to shared resources over which no individual or state has sovereignty such as fresh water, air, biodiversity, and, of course, the ocean.

As wonderful as this shared heritage and legacy might sound, we have thus far been slow to protect and preserve our commons. Most of the global governance institutions designed to do this are struggling. They need to be rethought, restructured, reorganised, and retooled. Luckily, the extraordinary age in which we're living—this Fourth Industrial Revolution of ours—offers ways of safeguarding our commons for future generations.

Back in 1798, the economist Thomas Malthus first proposed his famous theory of population and growth. In essence, he argued that human populations have the potential to grow exponentially (the rate at which they grow accelerates), whilst the rate at which food production increases stays the same (the rate is linear). When a population begins to outgrow its ability to feed itself, it is automatically checked—and brutally so.

Besides the differing growth rates of population and food production posited by Malthus, we have a more obvious problem. Even if the latter could keep up with the former, how could it do so indefinitely? What's more, the problem presented by our burgeoning population is further compounded by that population's lifestyle. Even though the growth rate is slowing and birth rates are starting to level off globally, the proportion of the global population living carbon-heavy lives of bourgeois domesticity and consumption is increasing. This is the trade-off at the heart of the ideological conflict between, on the one hand Malthus and his belief in natural limits to growth, and on the other, economists such as Adam Smith (1776) and David Ricardo (1817) whose work on labour specialisation, free trade, and comparative advantage describe a world of unfettered economic growth and innovation, limited not by natural resources but by human ingenuity. Human ingenuity, they argued, was not a scarce resource—until we started to hit against the maximum capacity for our planet to support life, with our current demands.

Few will argue that you can support infinite growth from finite resources. As Sir David Attenborough told the Royal Geographical Society in 2013, 'anyone who thinks you can [...] is either a madman or an economist.'

PLANETARY BOUNDARIES

Whether we're madmen, economists, mad economists, or none of the above, two things are clear. First, our global population is growing. Second, as economies grow, a greater and greater proportion of this population aspire to what those in the West might call a middle-class lifestyle. Both these facts mean that the demands put upon the planet's resources are increasing. One of our most important objectives is to reach a new definition of economic growth and uncouple it—as well as population growth—from increased resource intensity.

All over the world, more and more of us are driving more and more cars, using more water and electricity, heating or cooling more and more homes, and eating more and more meat and seafood. We currently demand more of the regenerative resources from the Earth than it can sustainably provide and produce more greenhouse gases (GHGs) from the burning of fossil fuels than it can absorb. We need, in fact, 1.5 worlds, or around 18 months of Earth's operating budget, for fresh water, food, and so on to meet our demands each year.

If we imagine the world's resources to be a bank, where once we were living off the interest generated by the capital, we are now working our way through the capital itself. As we do so, the amount of interest that the capital is able to generate is reduced. This makes living off it, as future generations will have to do as well, increasingly difficult.

It's predicted that by 2030 we'll need twice what the Earth can provide if we carry on with 'business as usual'. We are living beyond our means and beyond our planetary boundaries.

In 2009, researchers at the Stockholm Resilience Center published an article in the journal Science in which they identified nine such boundaries:

> 'Four of nine planetary boundaries have now been crossed [...]
> The four are: climate change, loss of biosphere integrity, land-system change, [and] altered biogeochemical cycles (phosphorus and nitrogen).
> Two of these, climate change and biosphere integrity, are what the scientists call core boundaries. Significantly altering either of these core boundaries would "drive the Earth System into a new state".'

We are also nudging the red line on several other core boundaries like ocean acidification and stratospheric ozone depletion.

In addition to all this, there are measurements where we don't even know where the red line is. For example, what is the minimum diversity of life required to make the Earth's biosphere function? Take another example: We think that the 'safe' level of atmospheric carbon dioxide is 350 parts per million but we don't know for sure. We do know, however, that it has already broken through 400ppm.

Nor do we know the maximum particulate pollution load the atmosphere can withstand. What is the impact of all the novel chemicals and compounds we release into the environment? We have a fair understanding of some of these such as industrial cooling fluids (like PCBs) and heavy metals like mercury, but the full impact on cellular biology and ecology of others, like plastic, are far from clear.

How we use the planet's resources and how our colossal population interacts with the world's life-support systems needs radically rethinking if we are to stay within our planetary boundaries and keep those systems operating.

TIPPING POINTS

It's more complicated than that, though. Even were we to live within these planetary boundaries, we may pass tipping points that lead to irreversible phase changes in large-scale physical and biological conditions on Earth. Simply put, the stable and benign Holocene conditions that have so far allowed us to prosper could soon become a thing of the past. In fact, so wide-ranging and so profound are the effects of human activity that some scientists argue we have already left the Holocene epoch behind and entered a new one. The name they have given it reflects this human impact on the planet, derived from the Ancient Greek words for 'human', and 'recent' or 'new': the Anthropocene.

Our oceans are a dynamic, non-linear system. This means that subcomponents of this system can appear to be ticking along well for years on end, changing very marginally, then suddenly hit a critical mass or tipping point after which they quickly degenerate at an exponential rate. On land, we can see this when we look at the effects of deforestation. Forests need a critical mass for each sub-system to interact effectively with one another. When we clear a path through the forest— to make way for a road, for example—we often discover that the smaller side of the forest reaches this sub-optimal state and rapidly collapses.

Sometimes these tipping points are passed quite naturally. For example, 250 million years ago a sudden, unexplained, and catastrophic drop in oceanic oxygen levels wiped out 90% of all marine species.

More recently and less naturally, we might look at what happened when we passed a tipping point just a few decades ago in the Black Sea. At the end of the 1960s, it was home to a healthy and diverse range of fish, crabs, sea stars, and plankton, all of which formed a finely balanced ecosystem reliant on stable conditions that had persisted for thousands of years.

Of the fresh water that drains into the Black Sea, 85% comes from just three rivers. Between them, the Danube, Dniestr, and Dniepr pour over 67 cubic miles of water into this delicate ecosystem every year—enough to fill Lake Winnipeg in Canada. The Danube alone carries the waste water of 80 million people who live along its length. In the 1970s, as industry and agriculture intensified along the banks of these rivers, huge amounts of phosphorous, nitrate, and silicate also ran off into these rivers, and then into the Black Sea itself. This was great news for the phytoplankton that thrive on such compounds, and for the fish that lived off these plankton. Fishermen saw their catch go up from 200,000 tonnes in 1970 to 600,000 in 1985, so it was great news for them, too.

However, all the fish that the fishermen were hauling in had been fulfilling a very specific function in the food web. In their place, the populations of certain carnivorous jellyfish skyrocketed. Over the same period, the biomass of these jellyfish increased from just one million tonnes to 700 million tonnes. Unlike the anchovies, these jellyfish have no predators. When they die they simply sink to the sea floor, where their decomposition draws the oxygen out of the water, further reducing the habitat available to fish.

Intrinsically, neither the prehistoric ocean anoxia nor the recent Black Sea crisis was harmful. It could be said that the harm done to certain species was merely an opportunity for other species to thrive and that both bodies of water would regain a new, albeit different, balance over time. The anchovies' loss was the jellyfish's gain.

This point can hardly be emphasised too much: the Earth and its oceans will continue to be just fine whatever action we do or do not take. Our struggle is not to save the planet. Our struggle is merely to save ourselves. And in a meaningful timescale.

This struggle means restoring and preserving ocean health in a way that allows it to supply us with what we need. Wherever we look, however, species and whole ecosystems are undergoing drastic changes. We are approaching and passing tipping points that are both hard to define and not linear, which means that we may not know we're passing them but, once we do, the changes become exponential and often irreversible.

Take, for example, fishing stocks in the North Atlantic and Mediterranean or whale populations in the Antarctic. Take the Great Barrier Reef in Australia or the marine systems within almost any industrialised port such as Singapore, Tokyo, Mumbai, New York, or Santos in Brazil.

Take the Gulf Stream that flows from the warm waters of the Gulf of Mexico across the Atlantic, eventually releasing its heat far further north alongside western Europe. Without it, the UK would experience Alaskan conditions and Norway would be as hospitable as Antarctica. The melting of the Greenland ice cap and Arctic ice could, in a matter of decades, disrupt the oceanic thermohaline circulation engine that keeps the Gulf Stream going. This is not a hypothetical. The Gulf Stream has already slowed by 30% in the past 50 years. What is more, our diagnostic tools and computer models are far from sophisticated. Among the many things we don't know is this: If it stops, when will the Gulf Stream start up again? Thousands of years? Hundreds of thousands? Never?

The Antarctic ice sheet is another example. It contains enough water to raise the entire global sea level not by inches but by hundreds of feet. Once it melts past a certain point, its decline will accelerate and quickly become irreversible. Then there's the deforestation in Amazonia, and desertification in East Africa. The list goes on.

Wherever we look, wherever we break through planetary boundaries or slip silently and unknowingly past tipping points, the effect on our global commons is likely to be profound. The conditions we find on the other side will be different, some of them hostile to human life, and many of them irreversible.

THE TRAGEDY OF THE COMMONS

The trouble with shared, unregulated resources like the world's oceans is that self-interest must be put aside by every party if they're to be sustainably governed and managed. Agreements must be made, treaties hammered out, deals negotiated, and compromises reached. This usually takes a great deal of time, effort, and political will. The approach tends to be hampered by some participants' assumption that they're playing a one-off, zero-sum game in which one party's gain is another's loss.

It's a problem that was famously framed as 'The Tragedy of the Commons' by the English economist William Forster Lloyd nearly two hundred years ago. He studied the 'common' grazing land that most villages at the time set aside for common grazing and noticed that when everyone acted out of self-interest the consequences were inevitably contrary to the common interest—and their own—in the long term. Overcoming this tragedy is an endeavour to which economists the world over are applying themselves to this day, sometimes to Nobel-winning effect as was the case in 2009 when Elinor Ostrom shared the economics prize for her work on the commons. She remains the only woman so far to win it.

Lloyd's observations present what in economics circles is known as The Prisoner's Dilemma, a famous thought experiment in which two rational individuals may choose not to collaborate even if it's in their collective interest to do so. Accused of a crime, they can choose both to stay silent and ensure a better joint outcome or they can confess, thereby optimising their own individual outcomes at the expense of the other—but ensuring a longer overall sentence. Invariably, most put their short-term interests first if this is their first and only offence. Things become interesting if they are repeat offenders or if they trust each other.

In Antarctica, the only continent with no human indigenous or local populations of people, we made peaceful progress toward solving the Tragedy of the Commons. The Antarctic Treaty came into force in 1961 and has been acceded to by 53 countries. The basic tenet is that Antarctica should be used for scientific research and off-limits to military activity and that any such activities cannot form a basis for any claims to land or resources (which were just beginning to be made at the time).

Although imperfect, it was brilliant in its simplicity and worked for two reasons. First of all, no one wanted to live there. Second, nobody ever seriously considered the possibility of drilling for oil or mining for coal and precious metals, all of which are thought to abound under a continental ice sheet that's anywhere between 1 and 3 miles thick. It seemed to work as intended and indeed it still does, essentially making Antarctica one huge protected area.

A more recent agreement which is part of the Antarctic Treaty System (ATS), however, has worked out less well. The 1982 Convention on the Conservation and Antarctic Marine Living Resources (CCAMLR) was designed to cover the resources of the entire Southern Ocean surrounding Antarctica. Because these resources are easier to get at that those on the land, there has been far less cooperation and it was developed after we began to fish in the Southern Ocean.

Governance in the Arctic is even more problematic because of the adjacency of powerful nations like Russia, the US, and Canada to the resources such as oil, fisheries, and shipping lanes. Nations have made claims in the polar regions of the north and there is no multilateral treaty that resolves resource use. Global warming is exacerbating the situation because, as the sea ice melts, oil extraction gets easier and cheaper, new fishing grounds become more accessible, and new shipping lanes open up. This has led to actions like when the Russian deep diving research submersible MIR dove over 13,000 feet and placed a flag on the North Pole, symbolically claiming it for Russia. The Canadians argue that they control the newly open water of the Northwest Passage, yet the US drives a ship through there without permission every couple years simply to set a precedent indicating that it is open international water.

Institutions like the UN that are designed to resolve disputes like these have often been born of tragedy and disaster. Global governance institutions like the IMF, World Bank, and various United Nations bodies and agencies would likely never have been established were it not for the two world wars.

Many of these institutions recognise that they need to adapt if they're to stay relevant. The world in which the victors of the Second World War, the five Permanent Members of the Security Council, set the global agenda, is no more. Now the G77 and non-OECD nations, particularly China, India, Russia, and Brazil, all have a greater say in the global leadership agenda.

The challenges that these institutions were designed to meet are often not the same challenges they face today. The tools they used to meet those challenges in the past are not the tools they'll need tomorrow. Many of the decision-making and implementation processes they rely on are no longer effective. With the pace of change accelerating as it is, with feedback loops getting shorter and shorter, why do we still wait years for a summit to be convened? Why do we wait months for a decision to be made, by which time the problem being addressed may no longer be the problem immediately facing us? Why are the transaction costs so high in getting the right leaders to the right meetings with the right agendas? If we're unable to overcome these shortcomings then we will need to develop bottom-up, 'seed & grow' approaches to complement top-down leadership and 'big bang' international agreements.

Of course, this doesn't just apply to environmental bodies. The governance of global security machinery, financial stability, global health-care, and even the internet face similar problems: Increasingly complex financial tools such as high-frequency trading and shadow banking are developing faster than relevant regulatory systems can keep pace; overuse of antibiotics puts us on the edge of a post-antibiotic world and at risk of a global pandemic; the Internet Corporation for Assigned Names and Numbers (ICANN) is facing challenges in maintaining the internet's stable and secure operation.

If all this seems like a crisis, then that's because it is.

But if it seems insoluble, take heart. Even if Malthus's theory proves to be partly correct, we can at least change our appetites and adjust our behaviour.

We said earlier that systems have safe operating limits. But systems can also be tweaked. They can be made to run on different fuels. They can be tuned, overhauled, and even re-purposed. Our ingenuity can ease the pressures we put on resources by delivering new and extraordinary efficiencies. New technologies can help us identify problems more quickly, formulate more effective solutions, and react faster.

Organisations can be reorganised and many of the tools they need are available today.

Before we get carried away and start tinkering with Spaceship Earth's life-support systems or rush headlong into wholesale reform of the organisations we've so painstakingly built up over decades, we should first ensure we understand the precise nature of the problem facing our oceans.

CHAPTER TWO

It is a curious situation that the sea, from which life first arose, should now be threatened by the activities of one form of that life. But the sea, though changed in a sinister way, will continue to exist; the threat is rather to life itself.

— Rachel Carson
The Sea Around Us

Life-Support System Diagnosis:
Declining Ocean Health

MANKIND'S RELATIONSHIP with the ocean is a very old and very complex one. Aside from the fact it makes life on Earth possible in the first place, it is also responsible for the relatively stable climate and weather humans enjoy, especially during the Holocene when agriculture thrived and fuelled civilisation. From the ancient civilisations of the Indus, Egypt, and Mesopotamia to the present day, water has always been central to human civilisation on physical, biological, even spiritual levels. The oceans have enabled trade and exploration, given up their food, and surrendered their fuel and minerals.

We now find ourselves on the brink of a more volatile time, the Anthropocene. If we're to stand any realistic chance of ensuring the ocean's future, we need to think of it not so much as a wilderness that needs to be restored but as a resource to be treasured and governed for the benefit of future generations.

We need to ask ourselves what we want from the ocean today and what we'll want from it tomorrow. We must define the pressures that are causing the decline in its health and understand what's driving them. Then we must work out how we can adjust our behaviours and priorities to mitigate the demands we make of it.

OCEANS MATTER

As science fiction writer Arthur C. Clarke said, 'How inappropriate to call this planet Earth when it is clearly Ocean."

Our ocean makes up the single largest, most contiguous biosphere on Earth, connected by a series of currents that run deep and shallow, horizontally and vertically, driving the water cycle and governing our climate. It's the reason that the Earth continues, at least for the moment, to provide such agreeable conditions for life. Indeed, it's the reason there's ever even been any life on this planet. That's why, when astrobiologists search for life on other planets, they look for water.

It is also central to all manner of specifically human activity back on Earth. Today, 40% of the world's population live within a hundred miles of the coast, 90% of all goods are transported over our oceans, and it's the last place on the planet where we gather wild food for large-scale consumption.

Until relatively recently, mankind saw the world's oceans as separate or at least individual entities. Even when we thought the world was flat, we 'sailed the seven seas,' mapping as we went. We made much more of a distinction between, say, the Pacific, Indian, and Atlantic oceans. It was a useful system at a stage when we spent most of our time wondering where in the world we were, where on Earth we were going, and whether we were going to fall off the edge of it before we got there. Today, however, and in a scientific context, these distinctions are less useful. It's for this reason we might sometimes refer to particular oceans but at other times to one large one: The Ocean.

There are several distinct anthropogenic pressures being put on the ocean. First, there's the issue of population growth and demographics. The global population is, it's predicted, in line to grow from 7 billion today to 10 billion by 2050. It's also expected that migration to coastal megacities over this period, many of them in low lying non-OECD countries, will eventually house 70% of the world's population along the ocean's 400,000 miles of coastline—a distance greater than that between the Earth and the Moon. This is a remarkable shift if we consider that in 2017, we have the same number of people living in cities as the population of the entire planet in the 1970s. Indeed, it was only in 2008 that for the first time in history we had more people living in cities than in rural areas. This trend shows no sign of slowing. Whilst much of the middle-class growth will be seen in China, India, Brazil, and Russia, the highest rates of population growth and urbanisation in the coastal zone will occur elsewhere. Low-lying countries such as Bangladesh, Indonesia, the Philippines, Pacific small island states, and along the large deltas of West Africa, will face a high degree of exposure to coastal flooding, so policies and adaptive planning for building resilient coastal communities are not only desirable, but essential.

Second, there is the awakening of the middle classes. The size of the global middle class is set to expand from 1.8 billion in 2009 to 3.2 billion by 2020 and 4.9 billion by 2030. The bulk of this additional 3 billion middle classes will come from Asia, where Asia will represent 66% of the global middle-class population and 59% of middle-class consumption (over double from today, according to the OECD). With seafood consumption per head higher in that region, we'll see an even greater impact and footprint of rapidly-growing non-OECD nations on our oceans.

Third, our technological and industrial progress is putting the ocean under pressure. New technologies and techniques are allowing us to go drilling for oil, gas, and minerals in deeper and deeper waters. They're enabling us to fish deeper, farther away from land and for longer. They're even opening up whole new sectors such as seabed mining.

Fourth, geopolitical change will have an impact. With the rise of fast-growing economies, particularly of China and those in Southeast Asia, the existing power structures that have so far governed our oceans will change and will need to be rethought as more countries lay claim to their share of ocean resources and define the global agenda on global ocean governance.

Then there's the issue of resource scarcity. As we look to mitigate the effects of climate change and as we start to run short of certain resources on land such as fresh water and food, we're turning to the oceans to find what we want. Although over 50% of our seafood is now farmed rather than from wild-catch fisheries, we are nevertheless seeing the collapse of certain species like tuna and cod out in the open ocean. It is also forecast that by 2050 water scarcity will affect over half the world's population—ironic in a planet that is 70% ocean.

OUR OCEAN In order to understand better and more accurately how all these forces make a difference, it's useful to look at where and how we interact with the ocean.

Coastal areas have always been our main point of contact with the ocean and where most of us have always lived and fished. The richly diverse ecosystems of mangroves, reefs, and seagrass are home to all manner of sea life; they protect our shores; and they also store a great deal of carbon.

Then there's the sea surface, where the gaseous exchange of oxygen and carbon dioxide that's so essential to our existence takes place. The photosynthesis that absorbs carbon dioxide and produces the oxygen also forms the base of the ocean's food pyramid and fuels the rest of the marine ecosystem.

The sea floor is an altogether more mysterious place with unique characteristics. For example, the tallest mountain in the world, Mauna Kea in Hawaii, extends 33,500 feet from the sea floor, making it almost a mile taller than Mount Everest. The more we study this strange world, the more we find it is not the barren underwater desert we once thought. It is an extraordinary habitat, teeming with life that thrives without light or photosynthesis. It's driven by processes that, due to the enormous challenge of working in such a hostile environment, we are still struggling to understand. The deep ocean is a dark, phenomenally high-pressure world that is variously cold and then super-heated to over 400 degrees centigrade around hydrothermal vent systems fuelled by heat from the Earth's mantle. While we are still in the early stages of documenting this world, we are reminded of the prescient lines from the 19th-century poet James Montgomery: 'A world of wonders, where creation seems / No more the work of Nature, but her dreams'.

The sea floor is already a vital source of oil and gas, and rich in mineral deposits that could be disrupted by mining. Like the sea surface, this is a boundary area through which chemicals pass in and out of the ocean. It is the sea floor, the sides of ocean basins and vents that makes the ocean salty and give it its chemical profile. The minerals in which it is so rich—as well as all the Earth's naturally occurring elements (most in trace amounts)—dissolve or are suspended in the body of water above.

Although we know far less about this boundary, we do know that it's an incredibly delicate habitat and one where a lot of human waste ends up.

The ocean itself is a body of water that is made up of a system of currents, absorbing, transporting, and transferring the Sun's heat, driving our weather, and regulating the hospitable climate we humans so enjoy. These currents are exquisite in both form and function. We can think of the water column like a layered cake with currents of different salinity and temperature heading in different directions comprising the layers. The system is driven by the physics of cooler, saltier, denser water sinking and warmer, less saline, less dense water rising. Like an endless conveyor belt, the currents rise and fall, dip and bob, and swirl around the globe in fantastical ways. The water is cooled and sent to the depths in high latitudes of the Arctic and Antarctic and rise to the surface and warming in lower latitudes near the tropics. It's an incredible journey, from the poles to the equator, with the trip for some of the water lasting up to a thousand years, moving ever so slowly, a time capsule, message from the past containing the purity and nutrients from a time long ago in the pre-industrial age. All of this movement and the temperature differences have enormous potential to meet our energy needs in the future, whether from underwater turbines capturing the kinetic energy of currents, or through new ocean heat systems such as Ocean Thermal Energy Conversion technologies.

In addition to these physical features, the ocean is home to 80% of our planet's living biomass and biodiversity. The colossal and complex ocean biosphere is not simply a source of seafood. It includes the largest animal ever to have live on Earth, the blue whale, and also some of the smallest and most mysterious organisms. All of these make up a complex, intersecting, and delicate biological system that stretches across the breadth and depth of the world's oceans.

WHAT IS CAUSING THE DECLINE IN OCEAN HEALTH?

The Earth's land, air, and water form one contiguous biosphere, so every impact in one realm has potential knock-on effects that threaten the stability and function of all realms. The cumulative effect of our interactions so far has been to make the ocean warmer, more acidic, and less biologically diverse. There are three major man-made pressures, or three 'Classes of Disease,' that are causing the decline of ocean health.

POLLUTION We're still learning which chemicals and energies are the worst offenders. Not least among them is atmospheric carbon dioxide. Not only is this a greenhouse gas, it also forms carbonic acid when dissolved in water. This leads to the dissolution of calcium carbonate structures like coral, the shells of oysters, clams, snails, pteropods, and the exoskeletons of crabs, lobsters, and other arthropods.

We also pollute the ocean with a huge variety of other compounds that stem from our industrialised lifestyles on land like chemical pesticides, agricultural herbicides and fertilizers, industrial heavy metals, human sewage, PCBs, and plastics, much of which runs into the sea through our river estuaries or off our coast after particularly heavy periods of rainfall. Out at sea, oil spills and sound pollution and even seemingly innocuous actions like the introduction of fresh water can all cause serious harm to ocean ecosystems.

OVERFISHING We are taking too much complex biology out of our oceans. In many areas, we remove more than fish populations can sustainably replenish. Globally, more than half of the world's fisheries are fully fished or overexploited. Some populations have declined by over 90% while others like cod and bluefin tuna in the North Atlantic have collapsed. Even when a fishery is regulated we often exceed the scientific recommendations for harvest levels. At the same time, illegal and under-reported fishing both mean that millions of tonnes of biomass are being illicitly taken. On top of all this there are destructive fishing practices such as bottom trawling that devastate habitats, and also the issue of by-catch, which refers to those species caught unintentionally in the pursuit of others and then simply dropped—often dead—back into the sea. Bycatch befalls any number of species including seabirds, whales, dolphins, and sharks. The impact on sharks, an animal type that survived the extinction of the dinosaurs, has now seen some populations fall by over 90% in just the last 40 years.

CLIMATE CHANGE This includes disruption to the climate system caused by the release of heat-trapping gases—most notably excessive amounts of carbon dioxide—into the atmosphere. These greenhouse gases have wide-ranging effects. Not only do they cause atmospheric and ocean warming, but they also change the delicately balanced chemistry of seawater. Since these pressures (and others) act simultaneously, ecosystems feel their combined effects—and the pressures are rising as the demands of a growing human population stimulate rapid increases in coastal development, food production, and industrialisation.

Some of these pressures have existed for decades. What is unprecedented, however, is the complexity, magnitude, and urgency of the crisis we face today. The impacts that we might have seen as local or regional such as coral reef bleaching, fish stock decline, pollution, and acidification are now global. One study estimates that oxygen levels in the ocean have decreased by 2% in the past 50 years, probably from climate change. Further colonisation and use of the ocean by people—for example, deepwater fishing on seamounts, deep-sea exploration for oil or minerals, open-ocean aquaculture, and renewable-energy extraction—means that soon, very soon, nearly every part of the ocean will be affected by human-caused pressures. Whole ecological systems are under threat, making large-scale marine extinction events increasingly likely.

OCEAN HEALTH AND WEALTH

Oceanographers who entered the field in the later part of the 20th century were immediately confronted with a crisis. With the ink barely dry on their graduate degrees, the ocean of Jacques Cousteau and *National Geographic* that they'd grown up with was changing so fast it set their heads spinning. Report after report came in that documented the decline and degradation of numerous species and ecosystems. Heads began to stop spinning when the term 'shifting baselines' entered the scientific vocabulary.

It all started with largely anecdotal accounts of how dramatically ocean ecosystems were changing. Scientists compared photographs of fish from tournaments and fishing boats from as far back as they could. The results were stunning and visually compelling. Where once thousand-pound bluefin tuna were caught near shore during the 1930s in

THE PARIS AGREEMENT ON CLIMATE CHANGE

The world came together in 2015 and produced the Paris Agreement on Climate Change. Governments agreed on collective action designed to keep the long-term rise in average global temperatures to within 2 degrees centigrade, and they are meant to aim for just 1.5 degrees centigrade.

These seemingly small figures may look like modest targets, but drastic action is required if we're to meet them without geoengineering. First, we would have to halve carbon dioxide emissions from industry and electrical grids every decade. Second, we would have to reduce net emissions from land use such as deforestation and farming to zero by the year 2050. Third, we would need to develop and scale carbon scrubbing technology so that by 2050 we are taking out 5 gigatons of carbon out of the atmosphere annually—nearly twice what the natural world is currently able to take out.

If we fail to do this, it's difficult to say precisely what the consequences will be. To humans, who tend to prefer stable and predictable climatic conditions, they would likely be catastrophic.

More generally, marine fauna and flora will move to follow temperatures to which they are evolutionarily adapted. As the ocean warms, whole marine populations will migrate from lower latitudes to higher ones. This migration has already started. Planktonic communities and some bony fish species are moving an average of 45 miles (78 kilometres) every decade. Shallow tropical coral reefs are particularly vulnerable to rises in temperature and will experience widespread die-offs. While some elements of these complex ecosystems will move away as the coral dies, the extraordinary reefs themselves, which have supported ocean communities and captured the world's imagination, could be functionally extinct within a human lifetime or two.

Since these target temperatures refer to global averages, in some places warming will be greater. For example, it is possible that a global average rise of 1.5 degrees centigrade could mean a regional 5-degree rise in the Arctic, melting virtually all the summer sea ice and sending that ecosystem into unpredictable gyrations.. This could be accompanied by massive plankton blooms followed by a catastrophic drop in oxygen levels, large-scale maritime extinctions, and, most worryingly from our point of view, disruption of the Gulf Stream. If average temperatures rise by 3, 4, or 5 degrees centigrade then our world will pass a tipping point into a hot, wet, wilder world that would, quite simply, be unrecognisable. Sea levels would be over 300 feet higher and super-storms a common occurrence, tearing through new coastal areas largely void of coral reefs or mangroves. It is impossible to make precise predictions regarding system as complex as the ocean when disrupted by abrupt change. We can, however, say that would be frighteningly and possibly fatally different from today.

the North Atlantic, for example, now the fish are typically less than 200 pounds and only found far out at sea. It was the same story with other species like cod, lobster, and sharks.

There followed a hunt for old photographs of ecosystems like coral reefs. Seasoned scientists from the 1950s and 1960s dusted off their slides and showed their younger colleagues what a healthy reef looked like back when they had studied them. The generation of divers and oceanographers above them could describe a reef from before under-water photography was even 'a thing'. They would inevitably describe environments that were even more robust than those in the slides.

The realisation dawned that everyone had a different starting point. Everyone had a different baseline from which they measured change in the size of individual specimens, the population sizes of the species, and the health of the ecosystems under observation. With new technology, we may discover what pre-industrial oceans were like, but there is a risk we may never know for certain.

There are, however, useful, objective, and practical ways of measuring the change in ocean health year to year. One such metric is the Ocean Health Index, a global measure expressed as a simple percentage. It reflects the ocean's ability to deliver a range of benefits to people both now and in the future. There are several activities to factor in such as clean water, biodiversity, carbon storage, food provision, coastal protection, tourism.

Other initiatives, like the WWF Wealth of the Oceans, valued the assets of the oceans and estimated the benefits we receive from them. The 2015 WWF report calculated this value to be $24 trillion in terms of direct economic wealth such as fishing, tourism, shipping, offshore energy, as well as ecosystem services like coastal erosion protection, biodiversity, and storm surge protection.

Whichever metric we choose to use, we must be careful where we set our sights. It will be a stretch to hope for a return to the ocean condi-tions of the pre-industrial era, within our lifetimes. The pressures on the ocean continue to be greater than the system can bear. Our oceans are dynamic and non-linear systems, so may appear to be functioning normally at first glance, but once an incremental tipping point is passed, could quickly lead to a series of cascading collapses. Our current interventions, as we'll see, are static and 'linear' relative to the challenges of a dynamic and 'non-linear' system. We continue to exceed our planetary boundaries, edging past tipping points and heading toward an uncertain, uncharted future.

Even if we put the problems of population growth, economic growth, or consumption patterns to one side, there can be little doubt that that industrialisation has marked this world-changing watershed. For nearly three centuries and over the course of as many revolutions, technological innovation has driven our increasingly resource-intensive economic systems.

We need to examine this extraordinary process of industrialisation closely if we're to employ today's innovations and those of tomorrow as a force for good. We need to see how this process changed our lives and our values.

TO REITERATE, this is not the death of the ocean. The ocean will be just fine in the long run. It's our own future that we need to safeguard.

CHAPTER THREE

*Turning points in human consciousness occur
when new energy regimes converge with new
communications revolutions, creating new economic
eras. When that convergence happens, society is
restructured in wholly new ways.*

— Jeremy Rifkin

SOURCE: McCauley et al. (2016)

Oceans in the Industrial Age

TO MANY PEOPLE, 'the Industrial Revolution' is a single historical event that happened a couple of centuries ago. To the 2 billion people who today have no reliable access to electricity, it's something that happened to other people entirely.

That historical event we know as the industrial revolution should be seen as just the first in a series. Each revolution ushered in a series of rapid technological, economic, and social changes. Each was driven by new innovation platforms and characterised by technological advances and accelerated economic growth that would change the way we interact with the sea for ever.

One after another, they transformed the societies they touched. The fuels we used to power these revolutions changed first from wood to coal. Then we moved from coal to oil and gas, and then to these we added nuclear power and renewables.

The materials we used would change, too. Having relied on wood and stone as building materials throughout history, we discovered how to mass-produce iron and then steel. Then we proceeded to unlock the deeper secrets of metallurgy. We learned how to make aluminium airframes, and we perfected processes by which, today, specialist alloys are not smelted but grown in crystalline form.

The discovery of other groundbreaking new materials like plastic, concrete, tarmac, and nylon would change our everyday lives as well as our industries.

Our mastery of glass would inspire profound revolutions in astronomy, navigation, and biology thanks to the telescope and microscope. It would also make photography possible and lead to the invention of television screens and fibre-optics.

Communications were also radically transformed. The postal and semaphore systems that were developed during the first industrial revolution would quickly be replaced by the telegraph, telephone, and wireless radio in the next. These would in turn give way to cell-phones, fibre-optics, satellite communications and a new era of connectivity characterised by the Internet of Things and machine-to-machine communication.

Transport, too, changed beyond recognition. From horses and carts, barges and sailing ships we moved to submarines, super-tankers, aeroplanes, and cars, and eventually to the autonomous, driverless vehicles under development today.

Fishing and agriculture changed too. They ceased to be simply a way of feeding and clothing ourselves and became industries of their own, supplying the raw materials for yet more industries. Industrialisation of these sectors fostered the development of pesticides, selective seed science, synthetic fertilisers, and eventually, aquaculture and genetic modification.

Even the institutions used to govern our populations were transformed. At the turn of the 19th century, limited stock companies allowed the early industrialists to expand beyond their personal wealth. Railways, colonial trade, electrification, and shipping were funded through opening shareholding and investment to other parties. As supply chains globalised and growth started to emerge beyond the confines of OECD countries, companies expanded to become complex, multinational corporations.

By the middle of the 20th century and against the backdrop of two world wars and the cold war, a new set of state-backed multilateral organisations emerged such as the United Nations, World Bank, IMF, GATT and its successor the WTO, the ILO, the WHO, UNEP, and UNDP, among others.

At the same time, a new wave of foundations and NGOs opened up and became a major force in the non-profit sector as society's values changed. This change was brought about by our full realisation of the enormous power we hold to disrupt nature. Our values have been shaped by the fearful images of world war, nuclear mushroom clouds, and our imagination of the awesome potential and fear of genetic modification, all brought to us via the medium of radio, photography, newspapers, colour TV, and the internet.

This change in values is not a new phenomenon. Values have shifted with every industrial revolution. Where once colonialism was seen as a moral imperative, human rights slowly but surely came to the fore, soon to be joined by civil, gender, environmental, and animal rights.

The current industrial revolution—our fourth in the modern era—is again opening new forms of institutions such as open-source businesses and exponential organisations. Once more, this revolution, these new technologies, new experiences, new institutions, will eventually shape our value systems in ways we cannot begin to fathom yet. We need to get out ahead of our ingenuity and for the first time allow our values, and not our technology to determine our future.

THE PRE-INDUSTRIAL OCEAN

Due to the colossal impact that they've had on the world over the past few hundred years, it is often perceived that our mastery of the seas has been due to the domination of European and Western nations. An uninterrupted line has sometimes been drawn from the Vikings, Ancient Greeks, and Romans through to Portuguese Explorer, Ferdinand Magellan who became the first to circumnavigate the globe in the 16th century, and onwards to the 20th century.

It is too often forgotten that for a thousand years after the collapse of the Roman Empire, there was the great Asian Ocean Renaissance. Navies from China, India, Japan, the Arab World, Indonesia, Polynesia, Micronesia, and Melanesia dominated the Pacific and Indian oceans, developing trade routes and advancing navigational techniques far beyond European nations thanks to their mastery of mathematics and astronomy. Naval leaders included the famous Chinese Admiral Zheng He and his six enormous fleets (1405–1433), who showcased Chinese mastery along the coasts of India, the Arabian Gulf, the Red Sea, and the East Coast of Africa; Arabian explorer Ibn Battuta who chronicled his voyages across the Mediterranean, Africa, and along the coast to South East Asia (1325–53); and the revered Korean Admiral Yi Sun-sin who successfully defended the Korean Peninsula from a far superior Japanese naval invasion force (1598). The 9th-century adventures of the Omani sailor popularly known as Sinbad; mathematical and astronomy advances in the Chola Kingdom of India, an important hub of long-distance trade in the 10th century; seafaring advances in Srivijaya, the name of the succession of trading states between the 7th and 14th centuries in modern-day Indonesia, demonstrate the rich maritime history of non-Western civilisations. Their hard work, intrepid exploration, and scientific zeal was marked by new sailing, seafaring, and shipbuilding techniques and all the adjuncts that would later be adopted by European navies, not least among them gunpowder.

The difference between this period and the last three centuries is the scale and speed with which the industrial revolutions have transformed human civilisation, touched so many societies, and impacted the entire ocean ecosystem.

THE FIRST INDUSTRIAL REVOLUTION *(1750s–1850s)*

The first modern industrial revolution can be characterised by transition from wood to coal as our fuel of choice and the discovery of steam power to drive our industries and our economies. James Watt's steam engine, patented in 1769, transformed production as well as transportation. For example, in just the half century between 1787 and 1840, British cotton production jumped from 22 million pounds (around 10 million kilograms) to 366 million pounds (over 166 million kilograms). While production soared, the costs of that production dropped dramatically. Turbo-charged industries like this needed people to work in them, so men and women moved from the fields of rural England to the cities, where they were put to work in the dirty and noisy coal-powered mills and factories.

This took place against the backdrop of the Napoleonic wars and naval supremacy by the famous British Admiral, Horatio Nelson (1758–1805).

On the ocean, the first industrial revolution would have an equally transformative effect. As the sail gave way to the coal-powered steam engine, trade was transformed as new and ever-faster steamships entered service. This led to a rapid expansion in the transportation of goods and people, and, as lighthouses were built and postal systems spread, international communication reached a level of ease and efficiency that until then had not been considered remotely possible.

It was an age of groundbreaking innovation. Science and knowledge advanced with the invention of the mercury thermometer by Gabriel Fahrenheit in 1714 to create more accurate measurement of temperature, and the development of the Celsius scale in 1742 by Swedish scientist Anders Celsius to standardise these measurements. This laid the basis for much of our meteorological work in understanding weather, climate change, and the linkage to our oceans.

It was also a time in which navigational advances allowed for momentous exploration and exploitation. European powers set out across the globe, charting the limits of the ocean basins, mapping their routes, collecting, prospecting, and, of course, conquering, colonising and planting flags as they went. North and South America, Asia, the Pacific Islands, the Indian Ocean islands, and even Antarctica were 'discovered' and crudely mapped out by famous explorers like James Cook (1768–1779), Charles Wilkes (1838–1842), and Sir James Clark Ross (1834–1843).

It is possible that the European technological and financial systems developed during the first and second industrial revolutions, which led to a military advantage over the areas colonised during this period, were the central to (or at least a contributing factor to) the North–South dynamic the world has today. Economists have debated the reasons for this. Some say it was the sorts of institutions and organisations created then (e.g., joint stock companies that allowed merchant navies to be built). Others put it down to innovations in trade and finance, again built off the trust implicit in Commercial Law. Either way, it is clear that mastery of the first two industrial revolutions led to almost two centuries of global dominance.

WHALING Although locally practiced for thousands of years ago in places like the Arctic, Japan, and South America, it wasn't until the late 18th century and the rise of America's New England fleets that whaling grew to be the first truly global ocean-extractive industry.

With its bright, smokeless light, whale oil was the high-tech lighting solution of the day, far superior to tallow candles or any other oil in the world. As demand grew and populations of humpback, sperm, and right whales declined in the North Atlantic, the whalers were forced to pursue their quarry farther afield, ultimately as far away as the Indian and Pacific oceans.

Alongside this expansion came innovations in at-sea processing that involved rendering the oil in large iron cauldrons heated by whale fat, an irony that did not go unnoticed by Melville when he came to write Moby-Dick in 1851: 'Like a plethoric burning martyr, or a self-consuming misanthrope, once ignited, the whale supplies his own fuel and burns by his own body.'

Advances like these, combined with the ships' state-of-the-art navigation and sailing technologies, allowed them to stay at sea for up to two years at a time. They would return to port from all over the world with many dozens of whale kills in their logbooks, hundreds of barrels of liquid gold in their holds, and enough revenue to pay all their costs, provide wages for the crews, and net a good enough profit to put the whaling ports of New Bedford and Nantucket in Massachusetts among the wealthiest towns in the United States in the early 19th century.

SLAVERY Whilst these whalers and sealers did indeed discover lands unknown to the western world, naming them as they went, they did not generally claim them for their own nor did they colonise them. Imperialism was not a business imperative. Whaling crews did begin press-ganging or tricking locals in the Pacific onto the boats and setting them to work, however. They called it 'blackbirding'. We might call it slavery.

Far exceeding the scale of blackbirding was the global, oceangoing, highly organised, highly profitable and completely legal trade in slaves and indentured labour. At its peak, the Dutch, Danish, French, Spanish, British, and Americans all got in on the act. The Atlantic trade triangle might start in West Africa, where ships would load up with hundreds of slaves packed like farm animals below decks. Those slaves that survived the voyage across the Atlantic would be sold in the Caribbean to sugarcane farmers. The ships would load up with sugar (or rum made from it), head to Europe, exchange their cargo for money or manufactured goods, and then head back to Africa to buy more slaves with the proceeds.

Similar systems continued after the abolition of slavery such as indentured servitude. This involved transporting millions of people from the Indian subcontinent to islands in the Pacific, Indian, and Atlantic oceans to work on colonial plantations that would feed and enrich the European empires until the system's abolition in 1920.

PIRACY Another dark underbelly of colonial greed was piracy. Though piracy has occurred since humans began using boats, the 'Golden Age' of piracy was in the 17th and 18th centuries, driven by the increase in traffic of valuable cargo—much of it associated with the colonies—to and from Europe. While pirates preyed on wealthy vessels of the French, Dutch, British, and Spanish colonial fleets wherever they plied the water, some local rulers employed them to maintain their domains, such as in the Straits of Malacca. Corsairs like Robert Surcouf (1773–1827) were French privateers who occupied the southern Mediterranean Sea, and made it down to the Indian Ocean where they terrorised merchant vessels of the East India Company. Notable women pirates included Anne Bonny, who followed in the steps of her lover 'Calico Jack' and practiced piracy on the Caribbean Sea, and Mary Read who disguised herself as a man in 1721 to join the crew of pirate 'Calico Jack.' Then of course there was the infamous 18th century English pirate, the so-called 'Blackbeard', who named the 'skull and crossbones' flag the 'Jolly Roger,' a flag raised to intimidate ships into surrender instead of fight.

NAVIGATION AND COMMUNICATION The problem of establishing one's longitude at sea was solved with the development of an accurate marine chronometer by John Harrison in the mid-1700s, giving Great Britain an even stronger hold over the seas. The British, along with colonial powers such as Spain, Holland, and France, went on to install further navigational aids such as lighthouses and buoys. They also drew up detailed charts of safe harbours and their approaches. The loss of life, not to mention the cost of losing ships, was a very real and very urgent concern to those wishing to rule the waves.

Intercontinental seafaring became less dangerous and more wide-spread as a result. The fleets and merchant navies that plied their trade across the oceans formed the first regular, global communication system. This global network meant that a distant colony or country could communicate on a regular (if infrequent) basis for commercial, personal, and imperial purposes.

THE SECOND INDUSTRIAL REVOLUTION *(1850–1950)*

This period was both a continuation of the changes of the preceding century and also a step-change, with a distinct inflexion in speed and scope. Social values began to catch up with the changes wrought by the previous revolution. Human rights came to the fore, central banks were established to govern a nation's finances, and there was a marked increase in state power and multilateral institutions such as the League of Nations and its successor, the United Nations and the Bretton Woods international monetary system.

This was also an era marked by unprecedented violence and ideological debate, a century after the Napoleonic wars, with the rise of communism and fascism, the industrialisation of weapons, two world wars, the Holocaust, and the start of the Cold War.

Innovations in fuel, energy, and transportation radically transformed our landscapes, economies, societies, and values. Coal gave way to oil and then to petroleum as the preferred way of generating power, and new ways were quickly found of putting this power to use.

The motor car would have the most defining impact on the 20th century—the century of the motor car—making regions closer, replacing horses, transforming agriculture with tractors as well as our urban landscapes. After Henry Ford began mass-producing the Model T in 1908, cars would eventually become a product of its own success and go on to become a major cause of environmental decline by the end of the century due to the impact of roads and greenhouse gas emissions from the volume of vehicles on our roads around the world.

Indeed, it is worth noting that Henry Ford himself acknowledged that he did not invent the motor car nor mass manufacturing. He simply put together the system to unleash the invention on the world. "I invented nothing new. I simply assembled the discoveries of other men behind whom were centuries of work... Progress happens when all the factors that make for it are ready, and then it is inevitable," he once famously said.

The Wright brothers also needed innovations in energy and the petroleum-powered engine to launch their new aeroplane into the sky in 1903, marking the dawn of a new era of powered air flight.

We would use petroleum to drive ships across (and even under) the sea. To this end, after many years of trial, error, and inspiration, the screw propeller was gradually perfected. For the day, having fixed blades turning around a central axis was a profound innovation and eventually replaced the side-mounted paddlewheels common of the era. In 1845, Isambard Kingdom Brunel's SS Great Britain became the first screw-propelled steamship to cross the Atlantic. Between 1850 and 1900, three British passenger lines—*Cunard, White Star,* and *Inman*—would dominate transatlantic travel, with ever larger, faster, and more modern record-breaking vessels like the *SS City of New York* (1888), *SS City of Paris* (1888), *Royal Mail Ship RMS Lucania* (1893), *RMS Campania* (1892), *RMS Oceanic* (1899), *RMS Mauretania* (1906), *RMS Olympic* (1911), *HMHS Britannic* (1914), *RMS Queen Mary* (1934), *RMS Queen Elizabeth* (1938), and the ill-fated *RMS Titanic* (1912) and *RMS Lusitania* (1906). Further propulsion innovations over this period led to more blades to screw-propellers and screw-propellers being added to vessels, resulting in the eventual replacement of the backup sail masts on deck, which had been a hallmark of docks around the world for hundreds of years. The ships themselves, for millennia built out of wood, would come first to be clad in iron and then made entirely of steel. These giant luxury liners would dominate transatlantic travel until the advent of commercial passenger air travel after the Second World War.

The discovery and practical application of another form of power—electricity—would also lead to a huge surge in innovation as the first electrical grids were installed. Electricity would drive assembly lines, keep printing presses running, and enable a new era of mass production.

Instantaneous, long-distance communication became possible, first thanks to the telegraph and the newspaper and then to the telephone. When Guglielmo Marconi used radio waves to send the single letter 'S' across the Atlantic from England to Canada in 1901, he demonstrated a technology that would go on to change everything from how we received our news to how ships could communicate with one another across oceans. As the passengers and crew of RMS *Titanic* would find out for themselves in 1912, Marconi's invention, which was installed and made famous by the fated ship, could mean the difference between life and death.

Overall and in the context of the ocean, this era was characterised by certain extraordinary feats of engineering. The process of laying undersea telegraph cables began in the 1850s and culminated in the trans-Pacific lines laid down in the early 20th century. The Suez and Panama canals were also completed at around the same time in 1869 and 1914, respectively, and would transform global shipping routes as well as dictate the rise and fall of new port cities. Both the telegraph and the canals required new technologies and new techniques, advanced engineering, and an almost unprecedented level of organisation. For those with access to them, these cables allowed for instant, secure communication unimaginable in the days of sail, just as the canals shortened trade routes and increased profits. As ship design improved, as navigation was perfected and as propulsion became ever more powerful, ocean speed records fell regularly over this period as the last of the great sailing clippers like the *Cutty Sark* and then even faster steamships plied their trades across the Atlantic and Indian oceans.

For better and often for worse, peoples and cultures were brought closer together, physically.

Our understanding of weather increased alongside our scientific discoveries, employing better methods and measurements, and more precise instruments. The Prussian Meteorological Institute was founded in 1847, the British Meteorological Society in 1850, the US Weather Bureau in 1870, the Bureau Central Météorologique de France in 1877, and the International Meteorological Organization (now the World Meteorological Organization) was founded in 1873.

On a far wider scale than ever before, humanity continued to embrace, explore, and exploit the ocean. Explorers ventured ever further into the Arctic and Antarctic circles, arriving at the North Pole in 1908, and launching famous expeditions to Antarctica. Mercator Cooper first arrived on that icy mainland in 1851–53. The 'Farthest South' record would be broken again and again in the decades to come. The Dundee Whaling Expedition (1892–93) would breach 63 degrees, Scott's *Discovery* expedition would pass 82 degrees in 1903, and Shackleton's *Nimrod* expedition would break 88 degrees before Roald Amundsen finally reached the Pole itself in 1911.

Less celebrated but highly practical advances were also made in other spheres, particularly in food production, transportation, trade, and warfare.

The fishing and whaling industries also embraced newly developed technologies. At the same time as they developed the technique of drag-net fishing, fishing fleets adopted oil-powered turbines, electric motors, and screw propellers to take them farther out to sea, for longer periods and to greater effect. The same innovations allowed whaling fleets to take new, more powerful factory ships into the whale's last refuge, the Southern Ocean. The invention of the exploding harpoon cannon in 1870 by Norwegian whaling and shipping magnate Svend Foyn ushered in a new era of intensive whaling, decimating stocks around the world. Both industries benefited from two-way radio communication that allowed them to coordinate their efforts and also call for help if they ran into trouble in these uniquely perilous waters.

Advances in oil-powered, mechanised, efficient fishing and whaling were soon made more widely applicable as, throughout the first half of the 20th century, western civilisation honed its ability to conduct wars on a global scale. The western powers set to work building air forces, aircraft carriers, and fleets of destroyers.

February 1906 marked a turning point as the heavily armed, hugely powerful *HMS Dreadnought* was launched, sparking a naval arms race between Great Britain and Germany. Just over a decade later, the world's first purpose-built aircraft carrier, the British *HMS Hermes*, was laid down in 1918, quickly followed by the Japanese *Hōshō* in 1921. It wasn't until World War II that combining the military capacity of seagoing vessels with the agility, range, and speed of aircraft came into widespread use. Along with the new carriers and expanded fleets, these same navies turned their attention to developing submarines to counter each other's naval threats. Pioneered in the First World War and maturing in the Second, this new class of vessel required that very latest innovations from a variety of fields. Diesel-electric motors and snorkels allowed submarines to move undetected, periscopes let them zero in on their targets, and torpedoes were developed in order to send them to the bottom.

This huge military buildup throughout the first half of the 20th century was not, of course, merely a western problem. Modern, mechanised warfare dragged in vast numbers of people from all over the world as colonial powers committed the wealth and populations of their entire empires to all-out war. As the battlefield spread beyond Europe, so did the environmental damage. Having given up so many lives to fight in foreign wars, many former colonies soon found themselves on the front line of the war at sea. These communities and ecosystems are still paying the price. Dozens of Pacific Island countries, for example, are burdened with hundreds of Second World War–era warships, submarines, planes, and vehicles that are now leaking oil and asbestos into the ocean, their unused ordinance growing ever more unstable.

Large investments and advances were made in all kinds of technology during the two world wars. Radio Detection And Ranging systems (RADAR), the first of which was developed in 1939, gave air defences early warning of attacking aircraft, and allowed warships the ability to see beyond the horizon whatever the weather, day or night. ASDIC (named after the Anti-Submarine Detection Investigation Committee) and SONAR (Sound Navigation And Ranging) came into widespread use during the Second World War and meant that warships could get a similar picture of the battlefield under the water, too. Systems like these, along with improvements in hydraulics and radio, would be put to more peaceful, profitable, but often ecologically destructive uses later on.

Technological progress relied, of course, on intellectual and scientific discoveries. The foundations of genetics and evolution were laid during this period, Mendel's study of heredity being published in 1866 and Darwin's *On the Origin of Species* in 1859. Lister first performed his system of antiseptic surgery in 1865, and Fleming would go on to discover penicillin in 1928. Our understanding of nutrition made comparable leaps forward, as did our systems of agriculture with colonial plantations around the world and new forms of crop selection, increasing life expectancy and supporting the growing populations of European empires.

THE THIRD INDUSTRIAL REVOLUTION *(1950–present)*

This period after the Second World War would see value systems shift once again. A wave of decolonisation swept across Asia, the Middle East, Latin America, and Africa. International institutions were established to accommodate this new world order. The World Bank (originally the European Bank of Reconstruction & Development) was founded in 1944, the United Nations and the International Monetary Fund in 1945. Bodies like the European Community, NATO, ASEAN, and the African Union (following its parent the Organisation of African Unity), founded soon afterwards, marked an era of regional cooperation.

As the global population exploded, doubling from 2.5 billion to 5 billion in just 40 years between 1950 and 1990, we would also see the rise of global campaigns dedicated to raising awareness of the fragility of our planet and supporting animal rights. New public-private partnerships developed between business, governments, and NGOs to address cross-cutting issues such as saving tropical rainforests and repairing the hole in the ozone layer.

Among the many technological innovations in every field from computing to seafaring, the Second World War would also unleash the awesome, awful potential of the atom. Its power to destroy cities and even whole civilisations would dominate the global ideological conflict of the next 50 years. However, its potential as a power source was equally revolutionary, not only as a fuel to generate electrical power but to drive ships and submarines in particular. The combination, along with advances in nutrition and innovations such as refrigeration and electrolysis, allowed Soviet and NATO nuclear submarines to spend weeks and even months underwater, often patrolling under the Arctic icecap because it brought them closer to their targets. This Cold War they were fighting would make ocean exploration more than simply a line of academic enquiry or a military endeavour—it made it an existential necessity.

As with the previous two industrial revolutions, the third might come to be characterised by certain new technologies and inventions like nuclear weapons and reactors, mega ships and supertankers, mobile phones and the internet. The tide of industrialisation was perhaps most obvious as concrete and tarmac (and then glass and steel) replaced bricks and cobblestones and gradually transformed the fabric of urban life. In the three decades following the Second World War, these miraculous new construction materials fuelled a construction boom. As economies grew, countries channelled their wealth into resurfacing their roads, building houses, dams, ports, airports, and power stations, and also drainage, water, and sewage treatment systems in mega-cities around the world.

However, at its heart and silently making this possible, lay another new innovation platform: the microchip and the integrated circuit. Over the course of just 50 years since 1959, television and cell-phone technology, PCs, fibre-optics, and the internet transformed everything from the way we worked to what we did when we clocked off.

The industrialised world at the end of the Second World War could be—and was—crudely divided up into US and Soviet spheres of influence. As the century drew to a close and the Cold War subsided, the G5 countries grew to prominence. Then the G7, the G8, and then the G20. The so-called Asian Tigers (Taiwan, Malaysia, Hong Kong, Japan, South Korea) grew rapidly too, adopting new technologies and heavy industries of their own as their populations demanded more and more natural resources to support increasingly western lifestyles. They were followed by other economies in the global South when, in 1967, countries such as Indonesia, Morocco, Nigeria, and Argentina organised themselves into the G77. Brazil, Russia, India, China, and South Africa, between them representing nearly half the world's population, followed suit in 2010, forming BRICS in order to give their collective economic interests greater weight on the world stage.

Even in the fields of medicine, biology, and genetics there were huge advances in discovering, then sequencing the human genome. It was only in 1967 in South Africa that Dr Christiaan Barnard performed the world's first human-to-human heart transplant, an iconic moment to many around the world showing the potential of modern medical sciences and also that such progress was possible outside the major Western nations.

The growing global population, the cities that grew up around the world to accommodate them, and the increasingly Western, consumption-heavy lifestyles that these expanding cities and burgeoning economies promoted all made new and ever-increasing demands on the ocean.

INDUSTRIAL FISHING During the 1950s and '60s, the whaling industry drastically reduced the last healthy populations of whales as industrialised fishing boomed. Fishermen headed to sea with new techniques and cutting-edge technologies. The miraculous invention of nylon, for instance, meant that fishing gear could be made stronger, larger, and longer than ever before. Two or three men with hydraulics and a good diesel-powered, steel boat could do the work of five or even ten men handling nets and pulling lines by hand. Later on, as satellites were launched into orbit to view the oceans from space, technicians sitting in their offices in Lisbon or Paris could direct their captains to likely-looking locations using the data that was beamed back. Thanks to pinpoint navigational accuracy, the boats could always find their way there and back. And with to ship-to-ship radio and satellite communications, they could even invite their friends.

The fish, like the whales before them, did not stand a chance. In the two decades following the Second World War, these fishing fleets caught as many fish as they could, regardless of species, and developed increasingly powerful ways of catching fish.

Drift nets up to 55 miles long were left to float across the oceans trapping everything within reach regardless of species. Techniques such as long lining and purse-seining were refined using nets the size of football stadiums.

By this time it wasn't just the human population that needed supporting. Fish were increasingly being used as feedstock to support the industrialised rearing of chickens and other animals. We also needed them to support yet another, entirely new sector—aquaculture.

Although humans across the world from Australia to China and Japan have been developing small-scale systems of trapping, breeding, and raising fish for thousands of years in shallow coastal regions, commercial aquaculture started experimentally in the 1950s and by 2014 had outstripped traditional forms of fishing around the world. Although we had been cultivating crops and farming animals on land for an even longer period, this was the first time we had attempted to tame the wild in any large-scale way with marine animals. The fish we were raising with this remarkable new technique, however, also needed feeding. And that meant catching more fish from the open ocean. The fishermen out at sea had no trouble meeting the demand—at least for a while.

It was not until the late 1960s and early '70s that they noticed a change. There were fewer fish to be found and it took more effort to catch them. Though apparent almost everywhere in some form or another, this symptom was spectacularly shown by the sharp, sudden, and catastrophic collapse of North Atlantic bluefin tuna in the 1980s and cod fisheries in the 1990s.

Finally, in the 1970s, governments began instituting rules and ocean resources became something to own. Although at 27 years old the UN was still a relatively young institution, in 1973 it began to address this global issue in earnest and, after nearly a decade of negotiation, the Law of the Sea was ratified in 1982. One by one, countries claimed their 200-mile-wide sovereignty over the ocean. Whatever lay within their waters, including the life that was in it and whatever there was of value on and under the seafloor, was theirs to preserve or exploit as they saw fit. Many had little knowledge of what was out there, but whatever it was, it was theirs and theirs alone.

There was a flip side to this coin. Rapid population growth was exerting additional pressure on agriculture. Farmers turned to high-yield crop varieties to meet the increased demand, but they also had to

intensify their use of pesticides like DDT and synthetic fertilisers rich
in nitrogen and phosphorus, much of which would be leached from
the soil and run down the nearby rivers and eventually into the sea.
The effect this had on coastal ecosystems soon became apparent in the
form of oceanic dead zones, most notably in the Baltic, Black, and Aral
seas as well as the Gulf of Mexico and many other places where either
rivers emptied into the sea or intense agriculture runoff was concentrated. Even semi-enclosed seas like the Arabian Gulf have not escaped
unharmed. The growth of coastal cities there since the 1990s had
increased the demands of desalination and power plants along a coastline—a coastline that is home to 45% of the world's desalination plants.
The salinity of the Gulf around these plants has risen by over 20% as a
result, which represents a major risk to marine life.

Countries that had establishing their sovereignty over these areas
soon discovered that, just as the ocean's bounty had become something
to own, so had the ocean's problems.

The Law of the Sea (LOS) treaty was the most ambitious multilateral
agreement in history, considered a 'constitution for the oceans' with 320
articles and 157 signatories. The LOS, which is based on an agreement first
introduced to the UN in 1973 and adopted in 1982, entered into force in
1994 and sets the ground rules and basic framework for governing over 70%
of the planet's surface. The world depended on it for determining ownership
of ocean territory and codifying the all-important Exclusive Economic
Zones (EEZs). The treaty also marked the start of a longer process about
how the world would manage ocean resources. While there had previously
been some ad hoc regional cooperation on fishery management, it was not
until the LOS and the 1995 Agreement Relating to the Conservation and
Management of Straddling Fish Stocks and Highly Migratory Fish Stocks
(UNFSA) that these became legal entities called Regional Fisheries Bodies
(RFBs), a diverse group of independent organisations of which Regional
Fishery Management Organisations (RFMO) are just one (albeit the largest)
type. What was not fully understood at the time, though, was how very
important the ocean was and would become to our very survival as a
species. The dialogue was about ownership, not planetary sustainability.

GLOBALISATION As the volume of our demand for seafood increased pressure on the ocean, the scope of our demands expanded as well. The global population exploded after the Second World War and we would need more than just fish from our oceans. We would need more and more energy to power both our industries and our modern lifestyles. Over just a few short decades since the 1970s, we would come to rely on the ocean for more and more of our fuel, with 70% of our new sources of hydrocarbon, wind, and tidal energy found on, in, or under the sea. Although oil-platform technology had been under development for decades, the challenges were considerable. It was not until 1963 that the first purpose-built semi-submersible, *Ocean Driller*, was launched. As the technique was refined, we set to scouring the sea floor off Nigeria, Brazil, Brunei, Malaysia, and plumbed the depths of the North Sea, the Arabian Gulf, and the Gulf of Mexico in our endless search for oil and gas.

Manufacturing, agriculture, large-scale aquaculture, and mineral extraction, running hot on all this oil and gas, grew and geared themselves toward feeding, clothing, equipping, and powering the colossal new urban centres that were springing up around the world.

Prior to 1955, dockyards were a hive of activity and cargo shipping was a haphazard process. A low-tech innovation—the humble shipping container—changed all that. It was a masterstroke that transformed cargo ships, lorries, cranes, and ports. With containerisation, automation, and robotics, cargo shipping changed overnight with super ports and mega-ships. The scale of efficiency in this industry is seen by the fact that today there are about 1.2 million seafarers in international trade worldwide who ship over 11 billion tonnes of goods a year, which means that less than one-tenth of one percent (0.1%) of the population move 90% of the world's freight over oceans that cover 70% of the Earth's surface; an average of 10,000 tonnes per seafarer a year. Automation helped turned one of the most dangerous professions, where loss of life was common, into one where safety is one of the highest concerns.

Reliable, affordable transport for these fuels and containers became more important than ever. Traffic across the oceans and through the great Panama and Suez canals ballooned. Container ships and tankers got bigger and bigger, their size limited only by the dimensions of these canals, hence the term 'Panamax'. The ocean became a veritable spider's web of shipping routes along which the outlines of the continents could be traced simply by looking at the paths of shipping vessels alone, such was the magnitude of activity across our oceans.

Ports were soon inundated, then automated, then expanded again. Those that were too small or inaccessible to the vast new vessels, like London docklands, were forced to close. Others, such as Rotterdam, expanded still further. In other places, from Dubai to Singapore and Hong Kong, new purpose-built and highly efficient mega-ports sprang up, such as Dalian, Tianjin, and Guangzhou in China. Whereas 40 years ago the top ten ports included European cities like Belfast, today six of the top ten ports are in China, accounting for 25% of global volume of shipping.

Circling high above, a new global satellite network kept the system neatly synchronised. Though the space race may have been powered by irreconcilable ideological differences between East and West, this technology that it spawned could be put to peaceful use. The first commercial satellites such as the *Intelsat 1* (nicknamed *The Early Bird*) went into orbit in the early 1960s, and the International Maritime Satellite Organization (INMARSAT) was established in 1979 to provide reliable ship-to-shore communications on the high seas.

The microchip—that technological wonder that would allow us to travel into space and to the bottom of the ocean—would also be put to a less glamorous but equally significant task.

Long before laptops and smartphones, silicon chips were silently helping us keep the global economy running. They even enabled consumer air travel that in turn allowed many island paradises such as the Seychelles, Maldives, Mauritius, Fiji, Tahiti, the Caribbean, and Bali to develop essential tourism industries that made the most of mankind's fascination with the ocean. Western tourists, newly rich in time as well as money, travelled the world with snorkels, surf-boards, and Self Contained Underwater Breathing Apparatus (SCUBA) gear in search of 'unspoiled' ocean environments where they would discover pristine coral reefs, abundant with colour and life.

These silicon slivers extended their domain into every sector, from factories, plants, and power stations to rigs and docks. Inventories and transport schedules were computerised, transport systems streamlined and optimised, delivery systems digitised.

OCEANOGRAPHY Among the countless innovations spawned by the third industrial revolution, one is of central importance to how we have come to appreciate and value the ocean. During the Second World War, a young French naval officer co-invented a little gadget called a two-stage air regulator.

Jacques Cousteau's co-invention might seem like a bit of a sideshow in the context of total global warfare—a satisfying, intriguing, and pleasurable sideshow, but a sideshow nonetheless. However, within the context of all the other technological marvels that put satellites into space and submarines into the depths, SCUBA gear would play no small part in laying bare the ocean's secrets and firing the popular imagination. It allowed people to explore the ocean for longer periods and with greater freedom than anybody had enjoyed since humans first gazed out at the sea.

Prior to its invention, diving underwater had been a dangerous, cumbersome affair requiring a team of two or more people to lower a diver into the water and hoist them out afterwards. Whilst underwater, air would be pumped down to the diver via a hose, allowing him to stumble along with a helmet and heavily weighted boots.

SCUBA gear changed all that. It opened the ocean up to the scientist, the amateur enthusiast, and the filmmaker. Just as seminal photographs from space would force us to reassess our place in the world, so this innocuous little invention would transform our view of the ocean.

Oceanography had not been a formal or organised discipline prior to the Second World War. As we'll see in the next chapter, the need to conduct naval warfare and the natural progress of science and exploration would give birth to the study of oceanography in the 1950s and '60s.

This new discipline drew on the combined legacy of the two world wars, the Cold War, the space race, and basic human curiosity. What we found in the depths would by turn astonish us, inform us, and ultimately terrify us.

SEISMIC DISCOVERIES Along with the initial inspiring discoveries presented first to fellow scientists and then to the public, modern ocean-ographers also made two of the most important Earth-science discoveries in history. The first was plate tectonics. Prior to the acquisition of detailed maps of the sea floor, the discovery of spreading centres and certain crucial samples of seafloor material, we did not know the planet's surface was a dynamic table of shifting continents. One theory used to explain the jigsaw puzzle–like match of African and South American coastlines was that the world was forever expanding.

A series of discoveries made during multi-month expeditions on the heaving decks of oceanographic ships sailing out of Scripps, Lamont Doherty, and Woods Hole Oceanographic Institute during the 1950s and '60s would solve the riddle. First, the discovery of 'spreading centres' that laced the seafloor like seams on a baseball provided a mechanism for the creation of new 'earth material' and the movement of continental plates. Then the discovery of 'trenches' that plunged to dizzying depths of over 7 miles provided a place for the 'recycling' of crust, where the crust was thrust back into the Earth's mantle. Finally, the evidence of the reversing magnetic fields of the Earth (which happens on average every 450,000 years) was frozen into the once-molten rock that poured out from the spreading centres, giving us a clock showing the movement of the crust away from spreading centres. The mechanism, the engine for shaping the pattern of continents on Earth, was basically a massive, slow-moving global conveyor belt rising up from molten, spreading centres and plunging back into trenches. The system, when it finally sank in, made perfect sense. We could project back and see what the continents once looked like, piecing together Gondwanaland, for example, the ancient super-continent that incorporated present-day South America, Africa, Saudi Arabia, Madagascar, India, Australia, and Antarctica. We can also predict what the continents will look like in the future.

The second paradigm-shifting discovery was made in 1977 at a location called 9 Degrees North, more than 700 miles off the west coast of Mexico.

Scientists had theorised about the existence of jets of superheated water, heated by the molten rock of the Earth's mantle, spewing out of the sea floor where the planet's crust is thinnest. It was only when the research submersible ALVIN encountered one at a depth of 8,000 feet that they could prove the existence of these hydrothermal vents.

What nobody had even theorised about, however, was a new ecosystem of life around these vents, based on the metabolism of hydrogen sulphide from the mineral-rich water. This was the first ecosystem ever discovered that was not dependent on the sun for its energy. Instead, microorganisms at its base consumed a chemical for food, and the term 'chemosynthetic life' entered the scientific lexicon.

This last discovery in particular changed the way we viewed all life, suggesting that it may have begun around hydrothermal vents early in Earth's history, though this question remains unresolved. It also gave astrobiologists new inspiration, suggesting that life might be found in even the most unusual, inhospitable environments on other planets, as long as there is water and heat.

After two centuries of industrial exploitation of the world's seas, oceanographers and explorers would finally come to understand—and then show their understanding with the world—the consequences of our collective action.

They would also help us to begin formulating our response.

THE INDUSTRIAL LEGACY

The first three industrial revolutions did not consist simply of innovation platforms and new technologies. The machines, factories, and assembly lines designed to improve our standard of living impacted our quality of life, encouraging us to work harder in order to produce and consume more—more fast food, more cigarettes, more drugs. Even television, designed to inform us, would instead come merely to distract us with its glow.

Our progress, such as it is, has accelerated. Even the rate of that acceleration has increased. The gap between the winners and losers has grown ever wider. No wonder then that what we might look back on as progress has, even at the time, bred uncertainty and fear more than hope. We need only look at Dickens' bleak Victorian England or the full title of Mary Shelley's *Frankenstein: 'The Modern Prometheus'* to understand these fears.

Similarly, Thomas More's pre-industrial vision of *Utopia*, first published in 1516, was succeeded and vastly outnumbered by more dystopian visions of the industrial age. Narratives from H.G. Wells' *The Time Machine* to Huxley's *Brave New World* and Orwell's *1984* were told by and about the predominantly Western societies that had industrialised the fastest, depicting new technologies and ideologies that, having been designed to liberate society, had the opposite effect.

These revolutions provoked profound social changes and shifts in the distribution of wealth and power all around the world, both between countries and within them. They have divided the world into winners and losers, socially, politically, economically, ecologically, and environmentally. They have divided us into East and West, First and Third World, Developed and Developing, North and South. They have divided us into haves and have-nots.

Deliberately or incidentally, these industrial revolutions encompassed, required, and promoted—amongst many other evils—slavery, indentured servitude, and child labour. They relied on and fostered inequality and exploitation.

This is why each one was also accompanied by a revolution, hard fought and harder won, in values.

The men and women who started these revolutions, who dedicated their talents to fighting these evils, often did so at great cost to themselves and those close to them. They risked ridicule, imprisonment, and even death. Many did not survive to see their dreams realised.

More often than not, these extraordinary individuals came from the losing side of history. They fought to make the winners revise their attitudes. They fought for a redefinition of 'progress' of the values we hold, the value we place on resources, and the value we place on one another.

Slowly, very slowly, our values changed. Colonialism gave way to the independence movement. The system of slavery and serfdom buckled to workers' rights, social welfare, civil rights, and (in theory, at least) universal suffrage.

Throughout the first half of the 20th century, ideological battles raged between left and right, between state-backed and private enterprise. After the Cold War, we seemed to reach a consensus on the middle ground. Domestically as well as internationally, this 'Third Way' that was built on evidence based-policymaking was felt to have marked the 'end of traditional left and right politics'.

Geopolitically, unilateralism gave way to international law and cooperation, spawning multilateral institutions like the World Bank, the IMF, and the UN. Economic power and the influence that goes with it shifted, too. More recently, from the supremacy of the nation-state and private industry, we've seen how power has shifted. Governments and supranational bodies, multinational corporations, and the Masters of the Universe of global finance have been able to work in partnership with civil society and NGOs in a complex multi-stakeholder community.

On the ocean, industrial whaling helped pave the way toward animal rights, just as unregulated fishing and mineral extraction are giving way to environmental rights, both concepts that would have been ridiculed until recently if they'd been understood at all.

Though the values we hold today are by no means universal and though different cultures still hold different sets of them, they are at least open to question. What we might ask now is this: What values do we, as a global community, hold dear today that might shame us tomorrow? What values do we not hold that we ought to hold?

How can we redefine what we want from the world? How can we adjust our definitions of progress and growth? How can we direct this new industrial revolution rather than submit to it? There is an opportunity now to balance what we want with what is available, and focus not on consumption and the standard model of economic growth but on societal and environmental well-being.

Such systems, however, do not merely develop of their own accord.

We can redesign and refine them. Values do not simply change. They have to be changed, and we have the chance to do that. New innovation platforms and technological progress alone will not address the challenges we face or solve the crisis of our oceans.

This industrial revolution can be accompanied by a values revolution in which individuals and organisations can lean in and lead the way.

Modern Industrial Revolution Innovation impact on oceans	Exploration (1750s – 1850s)	Exploitation (1850s – 1950s)	Degradation (1950s – present)	Regeneration (2010s – future)
Production:	• Traditional, net-line fishing • Harpoon whaling	• Industrial, drag-net fishing • Whaling factory ships	• Aquaculture (fish farms) • Coastal pollution	• Synthetic biology • Automated Aquaculture
Transport	• Sail to steam	• Oil powered ships • Submarines • The Container	• Megaships • Automated ports	• Autonomous Vessels • Subsea robotics
Communi-cations	• Postal system • Lighthouses • Semaphore	• Telephone • Telegraph/radio • Ship to ship communications	• Mobile Phone • Internet • Satellite Comms/GPS	• IoT /Machine to Machine Tech • AI/Machine Learning • Inter-species Communications
Natural Resources	• Wood to coal	• Oil/gas turbines • Electric motors	• Deepwater Oil/Gas Rigs • Renewable Energy (turbines and tidal)	• Seabed Mining • New Ocean Energy (e.g., ocean thermal currents)
Institutions	• Limited Liability Company • Role of Law/States	• Multi-National Corp • International Law/UN	• Open-Sourced Company • Public-Private Partnerships	• Networked, On-Demand Organisations
Human Population	• 1-3 billion	• 3–5 billion	• 5-9 billion	• 9-tbd billion
Terrestrial Extinctions	• 50	• 100	• 275	• Tbd
Marine Extinctions	• 0	• 10	• 25	• Tbd
Values	• Age of Colonialism	• Age of Human Rights	• Age of Environmental and Animal Rights	• Age of Ecosystem Rights
Power Structures	• Naval power	• Legal and state power	• State backed multilateral systems (e.g., UN)	• Networked Leadership

SOURCE: Degnarain, Davis, Graphic: McCauley (2017)

CHAPTER FOUR

*Never doubt that a small group of
thoughtful, committed citizens can
change the world. Indeed, it is the
only thing that ever has.*

— Margaret Mead

Knights in Shining Armour

OUR COLLECTIVE AWARENESS of and interest in ocean issues
has risen and fallen over the decades, the tide of global consciousness
governed by particular galvanising events and certain new technologies.
Nuclear tests and oil spills, tsunamis and shipwrecks, space flight
and water sports have all prompted us to view and value the ocean
differently and to address its problems in different ways.

Orthodoxies evolved, new doctrines emerged, and new kinds
of organisations developed alongside them. We've seen science-led
approaches to conservation, intergovernmental initiatives, and also
public-private partnerships that promote sustainable business practices.
We've seen mass movements enabled by mass media, and we've seen
direct-action groups—groups that have formed and been formed by
these movements—fighting for environmental justice. It seems like
we've seen (and tried) it all, in one form of another.

Part of the problem is that we've never viewed or tackled ocean
health as one unified subject. Most countries have never thought to
establish government ministries dedicated to the ocean, but instead
have allowed different aspects to be handled by different ministries,
departments, and industries, each jostling for influence and control of
the agenda. The priorities of different players representing the military,
agriculture, energy, the environment, and trade compete for time and
resources when the need for cooperation has never been greater. Over
the past few decades, different 'ocean doctrines' dominated depending
on the prevailing winds of the time.

As a new industrial revolution dawns and we look to the future of
ocean governance, we should take a moment to reflect back on what we
tried in the past, why, and what lessons we learnt along the way.

1950s: MILITARISATION OF THE OCEAN

The industrialised world's collective attitude toward the ocean in the 1950s was still, at best, naive. Outside of those ancient ocean societies that developed a more profound relationship with the sea, we still thought of it as a mysterious and vast wilderness. There was no sense that our activities could do considerable or irrevocable damage. Our understanding of and interest in the ocean was coloured by the military opportunities it presented.

Modern oceanography—the integrated study of the ocean as a biological, physical, chemical, and geological system that brings together the academic disciplines of geology, chemistry, biology, and Earth science—only really got off the ground in the 1950s' and '60s. It was not until this point that we began to explore the water column and seafloor systematically, measure large-scale currents, and dive underwater with SCUBA gear and submarines. Then, as satellite technology allowed us to view it from above, we started fully to comprehend the global nature of this salty, watery blanket that covered the Earth.

At the end of his presidential term in 1961, US President Eisenhower described the power of the military-industrial complex, that informal alliance between military and private industry, which drove and influenced US public policy over this period. It first began to manifest itself on the ocean in the form of rapid naval growth greater even than that of the Second World War. With the recent memory of how the Royal Navy shaped the British Empire's domination over one-quarter of the world fresh in their minds, the USA and USSR sought to out-manoeuvre and dominate one another with new submarine and ship technologies. Thus the Cold War heralded a new level of interest in the ocean, driven by military necessity.

Similarly, the extraordinary potential of nuclear physics to power ships and cities was first harnessed by the military for its potential to destroy them. Our scientific understanding of ocean currents and acoustics is rooted in the need for nuclear fleets to track one another. Those same acoustic buoys that could detect the subtle whirr of an enemy propeller could also be used to report whale song, an underwater earthquake, or any number of other natural phenomena.

It's ironic, then, if not altogether surprising that in the dawn of the Cold War and the birth of the atomic and hydrogen bombs lay the seeds of modern environmentalism. The shock of a full-scale thermonuclear weapons test in the vastness of the Pacific Ocean could be detected around the world, but in some respects the symbolic shockwaves were equally powerful.

Our realisation that we could destroy not just a city or Pacific atoll but our entire civilisation drew, as well it might, public attention. Images of palm-fringed nuclear detonations were as compelling as they were horrific, and changed the way that we viewed the ocean and our relationship with it.

1960s: CIVIL AWAKENING

The space race, like the arms race, gave us a fresh perspective. NASA's Apollo programme gave us iconic images such as *Earthrise* in 1968 and *Blue Marble* in 1972. Later on we would see *Pale Blue Dot* taken by *Voyager 1* in 1990. These allowed us, quite literally, to take a long, hard look at ourselves and to understand the fragility of Spaceship Earth.

Combined with the threat of thermonuclear Armageddon, this ability to explore space would provoke a cultural shift as well as a scientific leap forward, firing the public imagination and providing a much-needed sense of hope. If it lay within our power to destroy our environment, it was surely within our power to save it.

We should not forget that futuristic visions common in the 1960s showed underwater cities as well as space stations. The public gaze was directed downward to the depths as well as toward the moon. There was a sense of optimism that included a view of the ocean as a vast new opportunity, a new frontier ripe for exploration, research, and habitation. The first underwater habitats were developed, places where humans could live and work underwater for days, weeks, or even months at a time. Jacques Cousteau was filmed living in one, drinking wine with his wife, and predicting the future urbanisation of the oceans.

As colour television became mainstream, it brought these images and many others into our living rooms and we gained a new appreciation of the natural world. Among all the broadcasts and publications, it was Cousteau's distinctive, alluringly accented voice that communicated a new level of ocean awareness and, arguably, a whole new ocean conservation ethic.

The Underwater World of Jacques Cousteau was a landmark in ocean exploration, eloquently articulating his call for ocean conservation at the end of this decade. Colour photography and the growth of mass-market magazines like National Geographic also played a vital role in bringing the wonders of the ocean to life, as did Cousteau's landmark book, The Silent World (1953), Rachel Carson's The Sea Around Us (1951), and James Lovelock's Gaia: A New Look at Life on Earth (1979).

At the same time, Rachel Carson's Silent Spring (1962) revealed that we may have been destroying our environment as much as we were discovering it thanks to the far-reaching and poisonous effects of agricultural pesticides such as DDT.

Meanwhile, oceanographers continued their work, mapping the ocean floor and finally proving the theory of plate tectonics. Coincidentally, one of the oceanographers that proved this theory, Roger Revelle, also opened the door on anthropogenic warming from GHG emissions by proving the ocean could not endlessly absorb carbon dioxide from the atmosphere.

In a sense, we were rediscovering the ocean as we explored it, rekindling our love for it as we did so, as if reaffirming an ancient connection.

It was during the 1960s that we discovered that whales and dolphins have particularly large brains. One aspect of their brains in particular intrigued us—the cerebral cortex, that part of our own brain associated with memory, language, consciousness, as well as thinking about and planning the future. Surprise was no doubt matched by indignation in some quarters when it was revealed that the bottlenose dolphin has, in proportion to its mass, an even larger cerebral cortex than humans.

Cults formed based on this observation, and people postulated that dolphins were advanced thinkers and in some sense our oceanic counterpart. Research programs sprang up attempting to communicate with dolphins through sound, and their aptitude for training created a market in aquariums and zoos for dolphin shows. The military also saw the potential of these magnificent creatures and trained dolphins for warfare. In the harbours of Vietnam, the United States trained them to seek out enemy divers and kill them before they could place explosives on ships. The details of these programs remain classified.

No one was ever able to communicate with dolphins in any more meaningful way than we can communicate with any clever, trainable animal. No doubt their large brains are more dedicated to echolocation and social behaviour than poetry composition or philosophical musings. And this, of course, is precisely where our anthropocentric chauvinism was laid bare. We were measuring a dolphin's intelligence against our own rather than asking how well adapted its intelligence was to its environment. Our error is best captured in by philosopher Henry Beston in his book, *The Outermost House* (1928):

> We need another and a wiser and perhaps a more mystical concept
> of animals. Remote from universal nature, and living by complicated
> artifice, man in civilization surveys the creature through the glass of
> his knowledge and sees thereby a feather magnified and the whole
> image in distortion. We patronize them for their incompleteness, for
> their tragic fate of having taken form so far below ourselves. And
> therein we err, and greatly err. For the animal shall not be measured
> by man. In a world older and more complete than ours they move
> finished and complete, gifted with extensions of the senses we have
> lost or never attained, living by voices we shall never hear. They are
> not brethren, they are not underlings; they are other nations, caught
> with ourselves in the net of life and time, fellow prisoners of the splen-
> dour and travail of the earth.

1970s: CIVIC ENGAGEMENT

A decade of wonder and rapid technological change gave way at the end of the '60s to a sense of disillusionment and a loss of faith in Big Government. The student uprisings of 1968 and the civil rights movements in the US and Europe were all symptomatic. The Vietnam War, the Prague Spring, and the decolonization era can also all be viewed all against the backdrop of the SALT talks in 1972 and 1979 aimed at restraining the nuclear arms race between the two super-powers. Two oil price shocks, a series of labour strikes, the Winter of Discontent and stagflation (high unemployment and high inflation) created a tinderbox of disillusionment waiting to be ignited with the slightest spark. There was a general feeling that citizens needing to step up, make their voices heard and their presence felt.

The International Union for the Conservation of Nature was set up in 1948 to advise private, public, and non-governmental organisations on how to conserve nature whilst allowing for economic development, but more work would be needed to safeguard the oceans. Scientists had been warning of the collapse of whale stocks, for example, since the International Whaling Commission's 'Committee of Three' first reported in 1961, but it wasn't until a decade later that Greenpeace was founded with a $40,000 gift from the WWF (itself founded as the World Wildlife Fund in 1961, later renamed World Wide Fund for Nature) in the form of the now-iconic vessel Rainbow Warrior. This group of young European hippies had the beautifully simple idea of protecting whales by putting themselves between the whale and the whaler. Their direct action transformed the issue of whaling. It was no longer simply a question of sustainability but also one of animal rights. In so doing, regardless of how effective Greenpeace's approach was in terms of the number of whales they could save from the harpoon, they also focused the world's attention on the subject.

As Greenpeace modified and moderated its approach, other direct-action groups sprang up, employing practices that were just as dangerous and often illegal. The Sea Shepherd Conservation Society was founded in 1977 by a former Greenpeace member disappointed by what he saw as the organisation's aversion to aggressive intervention. PR-savvy as well as determined, the group became known for scuttling whalers in harbour, destroying driftnets at sea, and, more recently, for hounding illegal Chilean sea bass fishermen across the Southern Ocean.

As public awareness grew, so the scientific and conservation communities began to pull together in the same direction. The scientists' structured, methodical approach to defining the problems and proposing solutions harnessed and streamlined the drive and dedication of the conservationists. Our understanding of the ocean environment grew as oceanographers continued to fill in the large gaps in our knowledge. The discovery of hydrothermal vents was one such huge breakthrough.

Ocean conservation matured into an applicable science, the findings of which were impossible to ignore. This gave governments the evidence they needed to take action. As a more profound understanding of the scope and scale of the environmental crisis emerged, so public funding started to be made available. The US, for instance, passed the Endangered Species and Marine Mammal Protection Acts, and created institutions like the Environment Protection Agency and the National Oceanic and Atmospheric Administration.

This filtered up to the supranational level, prompting multilateral agreements and the creation of purpose-built international initiatives like the United Nations Development Programme (1966), the Stockholm Summit of 1972 which in turn led to the creation of the United Nations Environment Programme, and the International Seabed Authority (which was conceived in the 1970s but did not come into existence until 1994 with the UN Convention on the Law of the Sea). Dumping at sea—which used to be common until the 1970s—was banned by the London Convention on the Prevention of Marine Pollution (1972). Reports estimated that prior to the London Convention, over 100 million tonnes of petroleum products, 4 million tonnes of acid chemical waste, 1 million tonnes of industrial waste, raw sewage that was heavily contaminated with heavy metals, and over 90,000 containers of radioactive waste were dumped in our oceans worldwide. And this was only what was reported.

This increased enthusiasm for environmental issues prompted to further scientific work that would inform both the Antarctica Treaty (1961), and the formulation of the Arctic Environmental Protection Strategy that would form the basis of the Arctic Council (1996). The Whaling Commission's moratorium was passed in 1982, and the UN, after a decade of debate, finally reached agreement that culminated the same year with the signing of the UN Convention on the Law of the Sea. One of the most revolutionary measures from 1982 Law of Sea was introduction of 200 mile EEZs. Prior to this, territorial waters were limited to 12 miles (and prior to this defined by the length of a cannon shot, at around 3 miles). However, the tension between states with large navies and those that didn't meant those that didn't wanted more of buffer. Other tensions at the time were around access to narrow straits by those with navies compared with coastal states that wanted control of their waters. Similarly, the most productive fish were within 200 miles of the coast, and so many countries wanted control of these resources. When the UN Law of the Seas came into force in 1994, this transformed the management of oceans in many parts of the world.

The oceans continued to permeate our cultures and consciousness throughout the 1970s, not solely via the continued Jacque Cousteau TV series. Blockbuster movies like *The Poseidon Adventure* (1972), *Jaws* (1975), *Flipper* (1963), and *The Deep* (1977) mirrored an increased interest on ocean art and the blossoming of aquariums as a major weekend and holiday destination.

1980s: VIVE LA RESOLUTION!

A decade of disenchantment with state-led economic policies was followed by one that would see the rise of Reaganomics, Thatcherite policies, Rajiv Gandhi's market-based reforms in India, and the death throes of the Soviet Union. These events were accompanied by a general movement toward deregulation and free-market economics. Computing power advanced in the meantime, as did the number of applications for it, not just in the financial markets but in every industrial sector.

The gravity and variety of environmental issues demanding our attention grew in line with our understanding of the environment more generally. We started to see the bigger picture and to connect the dots. We realised that we couldn't just address threats to specific species; we had to look at the entire habitat in which those species lived. As phrases such as 'the ozone layer' and 'the greenhouse effect' entered the common lexicon, development agencies started for the first time to allocate resources to investigate and address the issue of climate change.

On the back of the Convention on the Law of the Sea (1982), further environmental agreements came into being in response to specific threats such as the Montréal Protocol banning the CFCs responsible for depleting the ozone layer that was signed in 1987 and came into force two years later. Such initiatives, however, could not simply be handed down from on high. Governments and businesses needed to work together to address these issues effectively.

Public awareness of environmentalism grew and so did a parallel interest in humanitarian causes. International aid in response to crises like the 1984 famine in Ethiopia became more widespread and, as we discovered aid's potential pitfalls, more sophisticated and more effective.

NGOs continued to fight the good fight, advocating for the development of the US Marine National Marine Sanctuaries Act. Private foundations like those of Pew, Packard, Munson, Moore, and Walton began ocean investments in the late 1980s and early 1990s, and the many smaller donations from a concerned general public began to add up.

The world's attention was also drawn to issues surrounding sustainable, long-term economic growth compatible with the natural world. The first female Norwegian Prime Minister, Gro Harlem Brundtland, chaired a four-year process at the UN World Commission on Environment and Development in what became known as the Brundtland Report that defined Sustainable Development. It was published in 1987, titled *Our Common Future*, and eventually created the momentum for the 1992 Earth Summit. Its targets were multilateralism and interdependence of nations in the search for a sustainable development path.

1990s: THE BIRTH OF PUBLIC-PRIVATE PARTNERSHIPS

The fall of the Berlin Wall and the collapse of the Soviet Union heralded a golden period of détente and a time, once more, of optimism. It was not only The End of History (in a good way) as Francis Fukuyama had it, but the End of Geography as well, according to Kenichi Ohmae.

Big, multilateral summits brought the environment and economic development into the spotlight. There was renewed hope and optimism after decades of living in the shadow of potential Mutually Assured Destruction during the Cold War. Our attention turned to new threats that faced the world. The Earth Summit in Rio in 1992 highlighted the major deforestation in the Amazon and widespread habitat destruction, and the Kyoto Protocol in 1997 focused on climate change and reducing harmful greenhouse gas emissions.

In 1992, the Convention on Biological Diversity (CBD) was signed, a multilateral treaty that among other actions to protect biodiversity, called on natural genetic resources to be protected for the benefit of all humankind. The 2010 Nagoya Protocol reinforced this convention as a partial reaction to the rapid advancements taking place in science that could disadvantage many economically poorer but biodiversity-rich countries.

The US National Academy of Science published *Understanding Marine Biodiversity* in 1995. Here, for the first time, they formally identified the five major threats to the ocean: biodiversity loss, overfishing, pollution, climate change, and habitat destruction. The disappearance of or damage to iconic species such as whales, sharks, manta rays, and sea cucumbers lay heavy on the world's conscience, as did several major global coral bleaching events, such as the huge underwater heat wave that in 1998 killed 16% of corals on reefs around the world.

The internet helped us understand that these changes to the marine environment were happening all over the world, not just in areas where oceanographers and environmental scientists were working. Television and mass media helped to publicise this discovery.

The contributions made by local and indigenous communities to identifying environmental threats finally started to be recognised about this time around the world in the Amazon, forests of Borneo, the Arctic, and Pacific Islands, as did their unique experience and insights into their causes and possible solutions. Ocean health was and remains, after all, more than just a matter of conscience to these coastal and small island communities. Their livelihoods and their very lives depend on it.

The vast oil spill from the *Exxon Valdez* in 1989 focused public attention on the oil and shipping industries. Aside from the huge environmental damage done, both were PR disasters. Similarly, in 1995, the issue of how to dispose of Shell's Brent Spar oil storage buoy put pressure on these industries to clean up their operations. Public perception mattered, public pressure mounted, and public relations departments had their work cut out.

New sustainable business models started to emerge. The shipping industry was forced to take responsibility and to regulate itself. Although the UN had established the International Maritime Organisation (formerly the IMCO) way back in 1948 to develop and maintain safety, security, and environmental regulations governing the shipping industry, enforcing these regulations had proved difficult. Though slow to react and easily sneered at, industry self-regulation can, as in this instance, be effective if an industry's interests align with those of the regulator and greater public good. Industry standards went up and safety measures such as double hulls were improved, leading to improved environmental protections. Unsupervised industry self-regulation eventually led to mixed results two decades later, where high-profile cover-ups took place in the fields of banking (2008) and vehicle emissions reporting (2015), forcing regulators to rethink models of earned autonomy.

An increasingly environmentally informed public made for a more conscientious breed of consumer. The fair trade movement grew in strength, and with it eco-labelling, certification standards, fair trade labelling of a variety of different commodity groups. As the decade drew to a close, people began to think harder about how and where their food—and their seafood in particular—was sourced and whether these sources were sustainable. This, of course, put pressure on retailers. More public-private partnerships were forged, such as the Marine Stewardship Council (MSC), founded in 1997 by the WWF and Unilever, whose job was to supply this information, certify standards, and govern this aspect of the supply chain.

However, whilst global awareness of environmental concerns rose, government funding declined. The United States' foreign aid budget hit an all-time low of 0.09% of gross national income in 1997, and institutions such as the World Bank and IMF encouraged all countries—OECD and non-OECD alike—to scale back spending in public programmes in a drive to improve government efficiency as a condition for receiving support. The results were troubling, with a lost decade of stagnation, rising poverty, and child mortality across many stretches of Sub-Saharan Africa, economic crises, and the threat of inequality plaguing much of Asia and Latin America. The anti-globalisation movement grew in momentum such that the World Trade Organisation had to cancel a major meeting midway in 1999, in what became known as 'the Battle in Seattle'.

2000s: "EVENTS, DEAR BOY, EVENTS"

The new millennium saw us move beyond the traditional boundaries of the public and private sectors as new actors and new organisations became more prominent. Private individuals, local communities, indigenous populations, scientists, artists, actors, and even religious leaders such as the Pope now had the technologies and media they needed to collaborate and make their voices heard directly. Thanks to sites such as Facebook, Twitter, Weibo, the will of the people—all the people—could be heard loud and clear by their elected governments—as unelected governments would find out to their cost.

The gap between the old political extremes of left and right that had dominated the previous 50 years narrowed further. Mainstream political parties across the western world jostled for position in the centre ground, but also reflected upon the progress and shortfalls over the past decade. This competition fostered a more rational, less ideological approach to policy making, and although differences were not exactly settled, they could more easily be set to one side for the greater common good. Cooperation flourished—

until the terror attacks of September 11th, 2001 that dominated much of the geopolitical agenda throughout the next decade, including lengthy conflicts in Afghanistan and Iraq, followed by a wave of terrorist activity that cast a shadow over many countries.

At the Millennium Summit in New York in September 2000, the largest gathering of world leaders in history committed to a new global partnership to end extreme poverty by 2015. The Millennium Development Goals (MDGs), as they became known, were agreed to by 149 heads of state at the United Nations Headquarters, led by the Harvard economist Jeffrey Sachs, and became the guiding framework for much bilateral and multilateral development assistance for the next 15 years. The MDGs would eventually secure $50 billion a year in development financing by the end of the decade, significant, but a fraction of their original target of 0.7% of OECD countries' GDP (estimated at over $40 trillion by the end of the MDG period).

The Kyoto Protocol came into force in 2005 and introduced experimental market-based mechanisms and new financial tools such as emissions trading. This spurred a whole new effort around innovative finance mechanisms to price and reduce emissions and hence influence corporate and government behaviour. New multilateral financing instruments were introduced. The World Bank–administered Global Environment Facility (established in 1991) developed new finance mechanisms for the environment and expanded its efforts to co-finance $60 billion of investments. The United Nations Framework Convention on Climate Change (UNFCC), which arose from the 1992 Earth Summit, established a $10 billion Green Climate Fund in 2010, with a recognition of the $100 billion-a-year investment needed by 2020 to abate the impacts of climate change. These complex, new framework agreements, such as the UN-REDD Programme (Reducing Emissions from Deforestation and Forest Degradation), were often impenetrable to anyone other than the experts. UN-REDD was followed by a more voluntary scheme, confusingly named REDD+, and also the Clean Development Mechanism as a financial tool for carbon trading.

Meanwhile, new forms of entrepreneurs and civil society developed their own tools such as the microfinance of the Grameen Bank in Bangladesh, whose founder Professor Mohammed Yunus was awarded the Nobel Peace Prize in 2006, to explore how grassroots financial efforts can support some of the larger, more high-profile international agreements.

As the decade unfolded, public-private partnerships were replaced with multi-stakeholder partnerships. Spikes in the price of food commodities and awareness of more acute resource scarcity such as access to fresh water led to the development of two multi-stakeholder partnerships, the New Vision for Agriculture (2009) that mobilised $20 billion into agricultural supply chains, and the Water Resources Group (2008) tasked with addressing water scarcity challenges, both incubated at the World Economic Forum and reflecting the broader range of stakeholders and increasingly complex world we lived in.

As new models of intervention, funding, financing, and research came into being, so ocean conservation was drowned by this cacophony of good and important causes to support. We weren't content now simply to save the whale—the conservationists' remit extended to include entire ecosystems. Scientific as well as public understanding of climate change developed quickly, as did our appreciation of its colossal implications. A worldwide financial crisis could hardly come at a worse time.

2010s: DAWN OF THE FOURTH INDUSTRIAL REVOLUTION AND THE POST-EXPERT ERA

The Banking and Financial Crisis would cause alarm, despondency, and profound disillusionment the world over as it became apparent that for the first time in history a generation would be poorer than the previous one. Major investment banks such as Lehman Brothers collapsed, leading to bailouts of much of the US banking and insurance industry. Cutbacks in the US were followed by a period of fiscal austerity that descended over Europe as the ensuing Eurozone Crisis and European Debt Crisis unfolded. First Greece requested an international bailout (and eventually became the first developed country to default on its debt), leading to a contagion of debt crises in Italy, Portugal, Spain, and Ireland which brought into question whether the single European currency, the Euro, would survive. This impacted not just Europe but all emerging markets and even China, which had been the major engine of global growth for the past decade and was now the world's second largest economy.

Beginning in Tunisia in 2010, many countries in the Middle East experienced a domino of social unrest that became known as the Arab

Spring, which led to long-standing leaders being toppled or civil war in Egypt, Libya, Yemen, Syria, Iraq, and major sustained street protests in 10 other countries.

The only respite from these crises was when world leaders came together mid-decade to announce a Post-2015 Development Agenda, known as the UN Sustainable Development Goals, as well as the 2015 Paris Agreement on Climate Change. These were the last major global agreements before an implosion of global solidarity and centrifugal forces started to tear apart the globalisation doctrine.

All around the world, as inequality continued to rise, social mobility was decreasing. Popular dissatisfaction and civil unrest swept across the Middle East before spreading eventually through Europe and the United States. The broad economic system that had carried us forward was starting to fall apart.

The perfect storm of economic slowdown, austerity, and social discontent led to short-term and populist political agendas starting to dominate. Political rhetoric and candidates in a variety of countries were running on a more populist, nationalist anti-globalisation platform, epitomised by the Brexit referendum and major election results in the US, the Philippines, and across Europe during 2016–17.

Amidst all the gloom, however, there remained a cause for optimism emanating from a small valley along the Pacific coast. Technology continued to advance and make possible growth and large-scale industrial disruption by companies that were once mere start-ups. Facebook, Google, Uber, TenCent, Alibaba, Weibo, WeChat, M-Pesa, and Airbnb had flourished by embracing complexity, Big Data, and a future they could scarcely have imagined when they were created.

This Big Data era could also aptly be called a post-expert era. The speed with which information is being produced is too rapid for any one person to absorb it, let alone master it. Politicians, academics, and specialists in every field are being challenged as a result because whilst the complexity of the problems facing the world increases, the public still demands simple, straightforward answers. This mismatch between expectation and reality has led to a generalised lack of faith in expert opinion, sounding the death-knell of the era of 'Government knows best'.

As the authority of experts is eroded, it's more common and far easier for non-specialists to contribute their knowledge and expertise outside their established fields. For example, wealthy philanthropists with an interest in a given subject but not necessarily a profound knowledge of it are questioning the status quo and received wisdom.

Oceans rose to the forefront of many leaders' minds with the BP-operated Deepwater Horizon blowout in the Gulf of Mexico in April 2010, leading to the largest marine oil spill in history. The environmental and economic damage was extensive, forcing regulators around the world to issue temporary drilling moratoriums and tighten regulations around offshore drilling.

As ocean health continued to decline, civil society was effective in mobilising a series of high-profile expert commissions over this period that engaged the great and good, and often non-experts in the oceans. The Global Ocean Commission—chaired by former Costa Rican President José María Figueres, former British Foreign Secretary David Miliband, former South African Minister of Finance Trevor Manuel—examined the High Seas. The World Bank's Global Partnership on Oceans looked at economic and developmental angle of oceans. The Ocean Elders, chaired by British entrepreneur Richard Branson, was established. US Secretary of State John Kerry led a series of major international conferences in 2014, 2015, and 2016 focused on 'Our Oceans' and public-private commitments. The Economist magazine launched a series of 'World Ocean Summits' to engage the private sector in ocean governance.

The economic potential of oceans started to be explored with a lens of seeing whether economic priorities could elevate oceans in the national discourse. China defined an ambitious agenda of a Maritime Silk Road, to complement its strategy of a new East-West land and sea trade corridor linked by a series of roads, ports, and large scale infrastructure investments. Small island states started to reframe themselves as large ocean states. Mauritius established a Ministry of Oceans in 2014 and Seychelles developed a blue bond in 2016 to raise funding for further ocean work. The Pacific Island Forum, a regional body consisting of 15 nations including all the Pacific SIDS, adopted the Pacific Oceanscape framework in 2012. The Pacific Oceanscape covers an area of nearly 15.4 million square miles, which is over 7% of the Earth's surface and about 10% of the ocean. The framework was first proposed by the government of Kiribati and aims to protect, manage, maintain and sustain the cultural and natural integrity of the ocean. It is the largest conservation initiative in history. The large-scale Marine Protected Area movement continues and hit a new milestone with the first high-seas designation in the Ross Sea in Antarctica (2016), and US President Obama designating Papahānaumokuākea around Hawaii (2016) as a large MPA, an area twice the size of Texas.

Formerly recalcitrant states such as Indonesia and China became more engaged in the ocean governance agenda, proactively taking steps to end illegal fishing activities. Further progress was made in addressing Illegal, Unreported and Unregulated (IUU) fishing with new satellite tracking technologies.

Major philanthropic foundations are also introducing new approaches to collaboration. With an endowment of over $44 billion, Bill and Melinda Gates' foundation alone is larger than the GDP of most developing countries. The Gates Foundation has a considerable impact on everything from disease control and agricultural development to nutrition and sanitation in over a hundred countries. It funds initiatives such as GAVI (Global Alliance for Vaccines and Immunisation), a public-private health alliance established in 2000, focused on immunisations and vaccines to save childrens' lives in poorer regions of the world. In the first five years of its existence, GAVI significantly increased the number of children worldwide with access to immunization, with over 125 million additional children immunised against hepatitis B, among other diseases. Initiatives such as this one have inspired other wealthy individuals to support them. Warren Buffett, encouraged by such breakthrough progress at the Gates Foundation in contrast to the slow pace of progress by governments and traditional development agencies, pledged $30 billion to the Gates Foundation.

The leadership of Gates and Buffett has spurred a movement around 'The Giving Pledge' that encouraged wealthy entrepreneurs to apply their skills and wealth to philanthropic causes by donating all their wealth during the course of their life. On the back of the successes achieved by GAVI in tackling an issue that governments, charities, the World Health Organisation and other established agencies had been working on for decades, it is part of new movement to attract private wealth to address other major global challenges to achieve radical breakthroughs. Set up in 2010, it has secured pledges of over $700 billion from over 150 of the wealthiest individuals on the planet, many being self-made billionaires benefiting from the third industrial revolution.

Others are looking into more new, non-traditional ways to harness this wealth—organisations such as the X-Prize which could tap into the broader range of talent that could exist outside of their narrow field of expertise. In 2004, X-Prize awarded $10 million to the first private space endeavours, unlocking an entire new industry of private space flight and changing US policy to allow private providers beyond NASA. This approach to rapid breakthroughs, hacking, agile teams, working to deadlines, 'failing fast', and rapid prototyping have shown that it is possible to achieve breakthroughs on some of the world's toughest challenges.

Although conventional power structures have had their authority and wisdom challenged, they are still very much on the front line in the battle to secure our ocean's future. Even as western politics starts to turn inward, the international community has nevertheless managed to forge the Paris Agreement on Climate Change and set the UN Sustainable Development Goals in 2015 as a grand vision toward 2030.

So the decade of the 2010s marks a period of growing awareness of the importance of oceans among global leaders with a series of summits and UN agreements that feature oceans prominently. However, the effectiveness of state leadership in many of these fora is being eroded by the general public's disenfranchisement with political leaders and the growing impact that technology is having on our lives.

LOOKING AHEAD: REGIME CHANGE

The multitude of overlapping, competing forces show that everywhere we look, we see dynamic, non-linear systems. We had earlier shown how our natural systems are dynamic and non-linear, and how the systems could quickly move out of equilibrium once we cross particularly important tipping points. We can now see that our economic and demographic systems are also non-linear, not growing at a stable rate but in fits and bursts, depending on events, stimuli, or tipping points. Even systems that are more challenging to measure, such as our social and political systems, appear to show non-linear characteristics, even in how quickly an idea is spread or behaviour is changed (e.g., car seat belt or anti-smoking movement in the West).

Our interventions, however, have been linear and static. Whilst they have been effective in the areas they were targeting, they were not effective at looking at the system as a whole and effectively switching direction of the entire, dynamically moving ship.

Looking across four metrics—time, degree of integration, multi-outcome, multi-stakeholder—many interventions in oceans have so far fallen short. The 'clock-tick' of our actions and time needed to reach consensus has not matched the natural 'clock-ticks' of the urgency of the ocean systems. They are rarely multi-outcome or multi-stakeholder, and it is rare that they are integrated across multiple systems (economic, environmental, social, political) in a dynamic, non-static way. There were occasions where we had perhaps one or two of the four, but rarely all four. We need regime change—regime change of the categories of interventions we deploy into the ocean, from static, linear interventions targeting particular sectors to dynamic, non-linear ones. We need interventions that have not been fully possible until now, at the dawn of the Fourth Industrial Revolution.

We have an opportunity to see the current state of flux as a way of expressing a new set of values and a chance to harden our resolve, to move forward deliberately using the currents rather than fighting them and being swept away by the tide. Spaceship Earth has one gear—'Go!'

CHAPTER FIVE

*May the relationship between man
and nature not be driven by greed,
to manipulate and exploit, but may
the divine harmony between beings
and creation be conserved in the
logic of respect and care.*

— Pope Francis
St. Peter's Square
22 April 2015

Teetering on the Edge of the Fourth Industrial Revolution

THROUGHOUT HISTORY, mankind has been bringing nature under control. We have mastered fire, crop cultivation, and livestock. We've discovered how to manipulate water to irrigate our soil and learned to drill for oil to power our engines and turbines. The Fourth Industrial Revolution could give us the tools to 'domesticate' even the oceans.

The innovation platforms that will power this revolution lie at the nexus of our biological, physical, and digital systems and have the power to turn societies upside down and inside out. Our systems of energy, transportation, communication and production are likely to be radically altered just as they have been over the course of previous revolutions. These platforms will significantly reshape tomorrow's business models and economics as well as the social, cultural, political landscape and our global governance systems.

But rather than sitting back and waiting to see what unfolds, reacting to the changes and trying to manage the fallout, there is a need to get out ahead and ensure that it is our values that guide our progress and not the other way round.

WHAT IS THE FOURTH INDUSTRIAL REVOLUTION?

Previous industrial revolutions liberated humankind from animal power, made mass production possible, and brought digital capabilities to billions of people. This Fourth Industrial Revolution is, however, fundamentally different. It is characterised by a range of new technologies that are fusing the physical, digital, and biological worlds, impacting all disciplines, economies, and industries, and even challenging ideas about what it means to be human. Whereas in the past machines were simply designed to augment our bodies and abilities, in the coming years they will be an extension—and in some case replacement—of our very minds.

DIGITAL PLATFORMS First, there have been tremendous advances in the fields of computer processing. Moore's Law, which states that the number of transistors in an integrated circuit will double every two years, appears to be holding true, leading to a continued exponential increase in processing power. We are even seeing progress in the field of quantum computing.

We're also making huge strides in how we collect, store, and interpret Big Data. According to Google Chairman Eric Schmidt, we've produced more data in the last two years than the previous 10,000, from a greater variety of sources in greater volumes and at a greater rate than any point in history. That's a revolution. It all needs storing, sorting, and interpreting, and we're quickly getting better—much better—at it as digital businesses the world over are proving.

Machine Learning, including the combination of artificial intelligence with deep-learning and self-learning systems, is another area that's maturing fast. We are being transformed by more sophisticated, lower-cost sensors, nanotechnology, advanced robotics, machine-to-machine operations, a fast-emerging low-cost nanosatellite space industry, cloud computing, fog computing, the Internet of Things, cryptocurrencies, and Blockchain and Distributed Ledger technologies on which these currencies rely.

We are, in fact, on the brink of developing digital technologies that will alter the very fabric of our society. These will unleash new, multibillion-dollar industries that will transform business sectors and economies around the world, transforming the worlds of finance (with FinTech innovations), supply chains, transport and logistics, agriculture and food production systems, and energy systems.

BIOLOGICAL PLATFORMS also have colossal potential to produce powerful, ground-breaking new technologies such as gene editing, CRISPR, and synthetic biology—technologies that raise as many ethical questions and they solve medical ones. This will free biomedical science from the need to harvest large numbers of marine organisms to obtain the genetic material on which they rely for research.

We may see widespread, lab-grown meat substitutes and new

plant-based energy sources. Some of these may not be high tech, but could be low tech such as the raffia grass bags used in many non-OECD countries until plastics arrived in the 1980s. However, we need to be mindful to avoid unintended consequences, such as the price spikes we saw in natural commodities as we saw with rice, corn and soybean in 2008, when these were seen as biofuels as well as a food product, leading to financial speculation. We may move away from pharmaceuticals and small-molecule chemical-based drugs toward new, large-molecule biologics and precision medicine. The possibilities are extraordinary and also endless. We won't just see treatments that extend life expectancy, but also the introduction of neuro-technologies designed to target and treat diseases beyond the blood/brain barrier. Procedures that were once the preserve of science fiction such as brain transplants and personalised medical programs under which individuals can have their own limbs and organs grown specifically for them may become commonplace—as will the ethical questions that accompany them around identity, affordability, and the limitless possibilities of our interventions.

PHYSICAL PLATFORMS New materials will transform societies. As we start to explore a circular economy in which there is no waste and where products are designed for reuse or to be biodegradable rather than disposal, we are looking at materials that could be a substitute for single-use plastics. 3D printing is already here—but what about 4D printing that enables us to produce objects that change state depending on the situation instantly and wherever they're needed, from space to the sea floor?

Allied to the digital platforms, our physical systems cannot be far from major advances in everything from autonomous vehicles, unmanned aerial vehicles, new miraculous construction materials like graphene, new energy storage and battery technologies, remote energy distribution platforms, and a new generation of renewables such as Clean Tech, solar and wind power, and the practical application of clean nuclear fusion.

Together, these platforms form a potent combination that's greater in scale, scope, and complexity than anything that has gone before.

A NEW ECONOMICS, A NEW POLITICS, AND A NEW SOCIAL CONTRACT

Although the difference between a short-term fad and a new wave of truly transformative potential can sometimes be difficult to distinguish, it is clear that the Fourth Industrial Revolution is very real. This latest industrial revolution fusing the digital, physical and biological worlds, is transforming every aspect of our models of organisation and—by implication—our business, governmental, and social models too. These changes are already challenging established assumptions. They're shaking the very foundations of almost every industry, radically altering the fields of transportation, hospitality, food, retail, communications, aviation, energy, construction, healthcare, and education, among others.

And remember—this is just the beginning.

'Sharing' is one of the new business concepts, whether that means sharing ideas, data, technology, expertise, or a ride to work. 'On demand' is another, referring to the ability of consumers and businesses to access people, power, products, and services wherever and whenever they want them, enabled by new mobile platforms. With a mobile phone and a modest line of credit we can book a taxi, reserve a table or a place to stay, order any one of a million physical products, listen to almost any music ever recorded, watch any film ever made, or access almost any facet of human knowledge. We can do this almost instantly and without even standing up or speaking, a concept inconceivable just a few years previously. It's an extraordinary condition to be in as an individual that is already posing profound questions about our understanding of concepts like privacy and identity. And this is just change along one plane—the digital field.

A new economics paradigm is being shaped by the Fourth Industrial Revolution. There are several lines around which the new economics systems are being defined. For example, access to services is increasingly valued over ownership of goods (e.g., ride sharing versus car ownership), distributed authorities over centralised authorities (e.g., blockchain versus central banks), abundance of services over scarcity of resources (e.g., on-demand education or health services versus fixed delivery models of limited school places or hospital beds). Models of smart network economics are winning over mass manufacturing economies of scale (e.g., micro-business ecosystems built around software platforms like Amazon, Salesforce, Alibaba, Facebook, Google versus wholly owned mass manufacturing supply chains requiring large upfront 'sunk cost' investments and high barriers to entry). This is making economic models possible that were once thought impossible. Network Economics—complemented with the Sharing Economy, the On-Demand economy, Distributed Authorities—inverts the laws of Demand and Supply of conventional micro-economics. Rather than demand for a service decreasing as price increases, utility and demand for a service actually increases as more users are added to such a system. At the same time, the marginal cost of adding additional users to a system is reduced to zero. Incremental supply can be brought online at almost zero marginal cost given the economics of the sharing economy. We are heading toward an economic model of zero marginal cost of supply. This means that these businesses can expand exponentially, as there is almost no cost of asset expansion given that the businesses do not own the inventory. We have seen this with Airbnb, Uber, and other similar digital platforms. This is radically different from the mass manufacturing businesses of the previous three industrial revolutions.

At the heart of this new economy is a new currency built around trust. Trust is key to making all these transactions function, and the more trustworthy a network, individuals or data in a system is, the higher the value it commands. The FinTech sector is hence transforming our means of exchange and even what we value in society. Gandhian philosophies of Swadeshi and self-reliance become possible with new forms of local digital currencies. The hollowing-out of the function of money will bring radical economic transformations as profound as when we created institutions such as banks, central banks, the Gold Standard, foreign exchange currencies, and even when we moved from the barter economy to a national currency system. Money as a storage of wealth, or means of exchange is being eaten away by a range of FinTech innovations such as virtual-currencies, social-currencies, crypto-currencies, peer-to-peer lending, blockchain, and distributed ledgers.

This, combined with progress in gamification, could allow consumers to have a radically new means of exchange, one based on values, rather than the value-addition or 'rent seeking' of each stage of production, which was the model of the previous industrial revolutions where each additional unit produced required a share of new raw materials, fixed energy and labour costs to produce.

Businesses and regulators that are adapting to the new conditions are thriving. Others are falling by the wayside. Another distinguishing feature that marks the new economics is that the phrase 'startup' has entered the mainstream lexicon as a respectable career path. Groups of individuals—often young, no more than mere students or university dropouts—are able to disrupt hundred-year-old businesses with not much more than a laptop and a few lines of code from their student dorms. This opens up the world to disruption from any quarter, any sector, any geography, any industry, any technology, whether related to your field or not. This opens up radically new solutions for our oceans.

A COLLABORATIVE COMMONS?

All this has far-reaching implications for how the Fourth Industrial Revolution can overcome the tragedy of the commons and create a new era of what Jeremy Rifkin describes as the 'Collaborative Commons.' Values can shift. These new business models can redefine how we govern our commons. Self-interest need no longer lead to self-destruction.

For example, conventional thinkers would have you believe that real estate of the everyday public street is a three-way battle between private cars, public transport, and pedestrians. However, with the rise of new ride sharing apps such as Uber and Lyft, we are seeing the start of innovative new business models. Similarly, when we look at hotels, they are being disrupted, not just by online booking agencies but by whole new models such as Airbnb where private citizens can rent out their apartments just like a hotel. Access trumps ownership. This radically impacts the decision-making and optimisation process, and gives the prisoner new options in the Prisoner's Dilemma.

Thomas Friedman quotes Tom Goodwin to make his point about

just how great and fundamental a change this is: 'Uber, the world's largest taxi company, owns no vehicles. Facebook, the world's most popular media owner, creates no content. Alibaba, the most valuable retailer, has no inventory. And Airbnb, the world's largest accommodation provider, owns no real estate.' Demand may increase, but there is much more efficient optimisation and a divorce of consumption from resource intensity of the system as whole.

DISRUPTION: DANGER OR OPPORTUNITY?

Everywhere we turn there are new winners and losers in this Fourth Industrial Revolution, just as there were in the previous industrial revolutions. Entire industry sectors are being disrupted. Of the world's largest businesses in the Fortune 500 list in 2000, only 50% were still there ten years later. The average tenure of CEOs has fallen to below a decade as decision-making in business, political, and news cycles gets shorter and shorter.

On an individual level, we're more connected to one another than ever before; one might also argue that we've never been more alienated. It has never been easier to share ideas and collaborate; it's also never been easier to spread extreme or destructive ideologies, either.

On a social level, we wield the power to augment and adapt ourselves on a physical and even a genetic level. We can print prosthetic body parts. We're developing ways to grow new, individually tailored ones. The potential for harm, however, is as great as the potential for good unless we treat ethical issues with as much respect as we do purely scientific ones.

On a national and international level, never have governments had at their disposal such powerful systems of insight into and control over their populations; then again, thanks to the internet, never before have they been so vulnerable to those populations they hope to govern.

In common with previous revolutions, the Fourth Industrial Revolution promises—or threatens—to challenge what we know or think we know about everything from transport, communication, and manufacturing to governance, privacy, work, and energy production and consumption. Are we, for example, going to unlock the full potential of small-scale nuclear fusion in the near future?

The coming decades will even challenge our ideas of what it means to be human as well as our morals and our ethical codes. Should it be possible, for example, to patent a human gene? Should your driverless car value your life more than a pedestrian's? If medical advances allow for brain transplants, do we come too close to playing God? What about predictive policing or prenatal gene editing?

It promises to alter all our existing power structures, disrupt business and government, transform our relationship with the environment and each other, and turn our values on their heads—and it will do all this over the course not of centuries but of decades.

It promises peace, prosperity, and equality. It threatens war, poverty, and inequality. And it has barely even started.

WHAT DOES THIS MEAN FOR THE OCEAN?

We must redefine our relationship with our ocean and re-examine how we co-exist with it as this revolution gets underway.

As discussed in the previous chapter, we currently have an intervention regime defined by a linear, top-down approach based on consumption and damage-limitation: we identify a problem; we try to design a solution; we discuss, debate, and draw up the laws and regulations to put that solution into action; we try—somehow—to enforce those laws and regulations; then we wait a little while to see if it's working; then we try again.

This, clearly, is not going be sufficient. Not with things moving as fast as they are.

To work effectively in our favour as well as that of the ocean, the next industrial revolution must, like its predecessors, also be a values revolution. Unlike in the past, we must try to define these values from the outset in order to guide the outcome rather than react to them at the end in response to a public outcry. We need positive values and thoughtful design principles that not only govern unintended consequences of new technologies but to also bend the arc of ocean health toward sustainability and restoration.

After all, if businesses and individuals can adapt and flourish under these new and extraordinary conditions, why can't governments, regulators, and international bodies?

First of all, there's a chance now to take an integrated, multi-stakeholder approach. It's difficult for individual leaders to address ocean health effectively in isolation. Governments are too unwieldy. Industry cannot be trusted to self-regulate without supervision. Foundations are not always accountable to the communities they serve. NGOs can be highly effective when it comes to innovation in specific domains but aren't always scalable; big, international NGOs (BINGOs) can become unwieldy, slow to react like the public services they sometimes replace, and often experience host country fatigue in non-OECD countries. The scientific community doesn't have the tools or influence to go it alone.

They all need to be brought together to form new, exponential partnerships that draw on the abilities and capabilities of every party.

Fourth industrial revolution technologies may give rise to new forms of networked leadership that were not previously possible and offer new forms of social justice. Whilst still grounded in partnerships with governments, the private sector, the scientific community, and NGOs, these new forms of leadership could also empower those who will suffer the most from a fragile ocean ecosystem, and connect citizens more deeply with our oceans. They need to be multi-stakeholder and multi-outcome, simultaneously.

We need to employ systems thinking. Rather than looking at each ocean problem in isolation or each technology as a compartmentalised solution for a specific challenge, every platform must be designed and integrated with the broader system in mind.

We also need to be more in synch with our natural rhythms. There needs to be a more proactive attitude to ocean governance. Historically, during periods of transition to new industrial revolutions, value systems were challenged and tended to lag behind, rather than be supportive of new technologies. Our future depends on ensuring that those employing these technologies do not just react to and accept the current governance systems, but have early warning indicators to proactively shape future governance systems for better stewardship of our oceans.

CHAPTER SIX

*The Gross National Product does not include
the beauty of our poetry or the intelligence
of our public debate. It measures neither our
wit nor our courage, neither our wisdom nor
our learning, neither our compassion nor our
devotion. It measures everything, in short,
except that which makes life worthwhile.*

— Robert F. Kennedy

A Vision for Our Ocean

New Values for a New Revolution

THROUGHOUT HISTORY, our individual and collective actions and mind-sets have been shaped by our values. These guide the trade-offs and choices we make on an everyday and societal level.

Over the past three industrial revolutions, our behaviour has been guided and conditioned by several forces, some sequentially and others in an overlapping and messy battle for influence. They partly account for the reason why our relationship with the ocean has ended up where it has today.

Historically, religion and religious norms have been a powerful force in many regions, guiding food consumption patterns and respect for living beings, or governing individuals' and leaders' behaviour. Our physical environment—the sea, forests, grasslands, and weather, and more recently our urban landscapes as the global urban middle classes have risen in influence—has also shaped many societies' interactions with each other and with nature. Over the last three industrial revolutions, the creation and access of law courts and the legal system has had a growing influence over personal and corporate actions as bills of rights, parliamentary democracy, juries of peers, and commercial courts replaced the historical need in some societies to take justice in their own hands. Abstract inventions such as economic growth and GDP have guided the decision-making conduct of many leaders over the course of the last industrial revolution, with a relentless focus on economic growth to overcome poverty and drive better outcomes for citizens.

More recently, the evolution of media over the course of the third industrial revolution from print media, photography, colour television, movies, and the internet, has pushed norms and shaped societal views and behaviour along a variety of topics. As we enter the Fourth Industrial Revolution, we are already seeing how new technologies such as social media are moulding the values of the millennial generation. We have witnessed the impact of Facebook and Twitter on the 'Arab Spring' uprisings across the Middle East in 2009, the breakdown of trust in governments with several major exposés by the whistleblower site Wikileaks since its founding in 2006, and rising concern around questions of privacy with a range of government and corporate hacking scandals of personal information over the past few years.

Each generation has been shaped by a range of influencers, based on the era they lived in.

As we enter a new era, it is important to ask questions about the forces being unleashed by the Fourth Industrial Revolution that could shape our values. What, for the better as well as for the worse, are the new institutions and levers of influence that will emerge? What roles will algorithms play?

AN ERA OF INSTANT GRATIFICATION

In the previous three industrial revolutions, our behaviours have changed. Technological and industrial processes have convinced billions of us to move from rural, agricultural-based villages to urban landscapes as industries and facilities become concentrated in urban centres. Jobs, electricity, schooling, and healthcare were more effectively delivered in cities, whilst at the same time agriculture was being automated. This had an impact across Europe and the United States and is spurring the current wave of urbanisation we are seeing in non-OECD countries around the world today.

Growing prosperity has detached many from the essential needs of shelter, food, and security (to take Maslow's Hierarchy of Needs) toward more middle-class pursuits of leisure activities. As society migrated from coastal and rural heartlands, the new urban middle classes have become less connected with nature and more connected with radio, television, the internet, social media, and mobile devices (and, we imagine, soon-to-be virtual and augmented realities). Media and mass communications have shaped our values, indicated by the battles for human rights, civil rights, gender rights, animal rights, environmental rights, as well as universal access to healthcare, education, and the internet, among others. The growth of e-commerce, mobile, and other technologies has meant that millennials are in an 'always-on' society, with an expectation of access 24/7 (e.g., e-commerce sites like Amazon and Alibaba), and shorter attention spans (e.g., 140 characters with Twitter; 10-second, self-deleting videos with Snapchat). As inequality has increased, with high youth unemployment in many regions of the world and greater barriers to home ownership, a younger generation's values are being shaped more by access than by ownership (e.g., access to ride-sharing rather than vehicle ownership, or temporary flat sharing rather than home ownership).

The horizon of decision-making at the world's leading businesses has collapsed, with shorter news cycles by which to react to a corporate story, radical transparency of a business—often by the media and customers—before executives have had an opportunity to fully grasp a situation, growing complexity and community of customers, suppliers, local stakeholders, NGOs and others that are impacted by the footprint of any particular business supply chain. Combine this with disruptive new Fourth Industrial Revolution business models challenging established firms, and many businesses' pursuit for relentless growth is being challenged, whilst at the same time shareholders demand results every quarter, which executives are accountable for in their daily decision-making.

Political leadership is experiencing similar challenges. Political and media cycles are also becoming ever shorter. From daily newspaper news cycles, to rolling 24-hour news, and now almost instantaneous 'tweets,' presidents and prime ministers are lucky if they can think beyond a week, let alone the next election. Decisions are scrutinised in near real time. In this era of shorter decision-making cycles and radical transparency there are fewer and fewer 'safe spaces' in which to pause, reflect, and experiment.

As a result, leadership has become more an exercise in risk-averse precautionary measures and reactions than in bold visions and risk-taking to forge new agendas. As Klaus Schwab of the World

Economic Forum is fond of saying, we are seeing many leaders who are solely responsive and reliant on their 'radar systems' to guide them through leadership journey, whereas what we also need today are leaders equipped with a 'compass' of values and vision to lead their organisations and societies toward a world that works for all.

What is the net result for our oceans?

In many instances, it has been left to civil society to address the plight of our oceans, which has successfully raised awareness around whaling, damaging fishing practices, coral bleaching, and oil spills. But on the whole, our planet has a heterogeneous range of values that shape different cultures' relationship with our oceans. Communities in many small islands are more connected with the sea and engage with marine nature every day; some cultures like Japan and Iceland have long-standing but different value systems than those of the urban middle classes of the West; and some cultures in China and South Korea are dominated by inland cultural beliefs that dictate the use and consumption of ocean resources even if consumers are detached from the processes and the complex supply chains that extract these resources from our seas.

Even in the West, many of the influential urban middle classes are further removed from a day-to-day connection with our oceans and, despite the occasional media attention highlighting particular issues, oceans and the planet are not fully ingrained in their actions nor in the revealed preferences of the masses (as opposed to their stated preferences in online surveys, opinion polls, and social media posts).

Unpacking this further, such differing behaviours and values toward the same ocean can be explained through the lens by which these communities view our seas. For some, the oceans matter for the environment, for the beauty and joy they experience when they surround themselves with nature and remove themselves from the daily grind of work. For others, their relationship is driven by food safety and the health and welfare benefits of consuming certain products from the sea. For others, there is a deep historical and cultural affinity with the oceans that define their very identity. For some national decision-makers, the oceans are a matter of national security, a buffer from foreign threats. For others, it is economic security, jobs, and the economic value contained under the waves that drives behaviour.

Whilst many of the strategies to turn around the use of our oceans are important, we will not succeed in the long term unless we are also able to reshape the values of the majority and foster a greater connection with our oceans.

All of us had a stronger connection with the oceans at one stage, and some societies still retain this connection. Let us turn to explore the nature of this strong, primordial, and spiritual connection.

THE OCEAN AND OUR COLLECTIVE SOUL

Whenever we look to our past or present-day cultures that have uninterrupted links to a sustainable relationship with the ocean, we see that wherever we look, the ocean and water have always had a special significance to them. Even some Pacific Islanders refer to islands and dry land as 'holes in our ocean.' The ocean forms the basis for the entire planetary 'hydrosphere': Water on Earth is locked in a perpetual cycle of evaporation from the ocean as pure distilled water, transported in clouds for redeposition on land and sea. The water that flows on land then rejoins the ocean along with the minerals and salts of which it becomes so richly comprised. When you view the water cycle in this grandiose way, the ocean starts in the clouds, extends down every mountain and river and into the sea. And the magic ingredient is the remarkable water molecule. Water, the universal solvent, is capable of dissolving more different things than any other known liquid, and it is the only substance that exists in all three of its 'phase' states (solid, liquid and gas) on Earth.

These remarkable qualities of water did not go unnoticed by ancient humans who, throughout the course of their lives, saw how important water was. Their understanding was based on empirical experience and knowledge rather than from the scientific understanding we have today.

The high value they placed on water is represented in the dizzying array of ancient water and ocean gods found in almost every ancient culture for which there is a record, ranging from the Greek and Roman to Slavic, Hebrew, Korean, and Filipino. The Chinese, for example, had Mazu, the Fujianese shamaness and Yu-Kiang, who ruled the sea in the form of a whale with arms and legs. Australian Aboriginal mythology has Eingana, a creator goddess and the mother of all water animals as well as humans. Ezili, in Benin mythology, is the goddess of sweet water, beauty, and love. The Norse, Germanic, and Celtic peoples also all have their own aquatic connections to the metaphysical.

The biblical story of Noah and the great flood, for example, shows water as a powerful destroyer, cleansing the Earth of the evil and disobedient. Then again, water is also portrayed as a great giver of life in many beliefs and is widely considered sacred: the Ganges River in India is held to be a goddess by Hindus, her waters making the land fertile and washing away the sins of humanity.

No lesser leader than President John F. Kennedy poetically described his connection to the seas in 1962.

> I really don't know why it is that all of us are so committed to the sea, except I think... it is because we all came from the sea. And it is an interesting biological fact that all of us have, in our veins, the exact same percentage of salt in our blood that exists in the ocean, and, therefore, we have salt in our blood, in our sweat, in our tears. We are tied to the ocean. And when we go back to the sea, whether it is to sail or to watch it, we are going back to whence we came.

These coincidences still remain one of the great mysteries of modern science, intertwined with the myths of origin.

Some scientists speculate that life probably originated in the ocean 3.5 billion years ago and did not come ashore for another 3 billion years after that. During this time, life became dependent on the ocean minerals and salts, so when the first animals left the oceans to occupy land they 'carried the ocean' with them, as it were, in the form of salty blood and cellular fluids. This ancient ocean in our blood is still a vital part of us and all other animals. Humans need salt to survive for a range of biological functions.

Ancient cultures may not have known this science but had a reverence for salt. In Roman times, the barbarians would accept salt as pay for service in the Roman Army, hence the expression that a man is 'worth his salt', and it follows that the Latin root for the modern word 'salary' is salt. It is not surprising that salt became so highly prized, and that its main source—our oceans—were so revered.

Take a deeper dive into any of these ancient or ocean-linked cultures, and you will see how deep the relationship with the ocean goes. For example, the Gilbert Islanders report a strong connection to 'Dolphin Callers' in certain communities. These individuals are said to have the ability to call dolphins into the lagoon during times of famine. After several days of fasting and meditating on the part of the caller, dolphins would strand themselves on the beach, presumably sacrificing themselves to the community. This was described by Sir Arthur Grimble, a scholar and resident colonial administrator in the early 20th century, in his popular autobiographical book *A Pattern of Islands* (1952) that was lauded as an important cultural account of these islands just after European contact. Putting aside the obvious question as to the veracity of Grimble's account, the point here is that these cultures are filled with respectful legends, myths, and association with the ocean.

Similarly, the New Zealand Maori embedded a spiritual connection to whales with their oral histories, which describe how they came to New Zealand 'on the backs of seven whales'. Some anthropologists speculate whether this legend represents six waves of migration in canoes, translated over time to totem animals such as these whales.

In furtherance of their attempt to capture how important the ocean is, such cultures frequently developed a belief in such totem animals, those wild creatures that connect people to the spirit world. In some ancient and modern Micronesian communities, for example, each person has a corresponding individual totem animal in the ocean. Their rules and customs were rooted in the belief that sea creatures were owed a respect and care, and violating that duty would lead to misfortune.

The Native American Iroquois people who today straddle the Canadian–United States border and are comprised of the six nations of the Mohawk, Onondaga, Oneida, Cayuga, Seneca, and Tuscarora people, developed a concept in *The Constitution of the Iroquois Nation* that has become known as Seven Generation Stewardship. This charter encourages long-term thinking not just on environmental issues but in every aspect of life:

> *In all of your deliberations in the Confederate Council, in your efforts at law making, in all your official acts, self-interest shall be cast into oblivion. Cast not over your shoulder behind you the warnings of the nephews and nieces should they chide you for any error or wrong you may do, but return to the way of the Great Law which is just and right. Look and listen for the welfare of the whole people and have always in view not only the past and present but also the coming generations, even those whose faces are yet beneath the surface of the ground—the unborn of the future Nation.*

With today's demographics, this would take us to thinking 150 years into the future. Is there a way to adopt a similar system today, maybe broader and perhaps more complex, but equally thoughtful, forward looking and sustainable?

THE PRICE OF EVERYTHING BUT THE VALUE OF NOTHING

Assuming we are able to shift the values of society, how can these be manifest in daily decisions, choices, and behaviours of individuals, society, business, and political leadership?

First, let's understand what has driven leadership and core decision-making, particularly over the third industrial revolution where we redefined our relationship with the oceans, and our planet, to become more extractive on a scale never before imagined.

GDP, or Gross Domestic Product, is an invention of the third industrial revolution. In response to the Great Depression and the paucity and fragmented pieces of data from which presidents Hoover and Roosevelt were expected to design policy responses, the US Congress commissioned economist and eventual Nobel Prize winner Simon Kuznets to develop a system to capture all economic production by individuals, companies, and the government into a single measure. This measure was designed to rise in good times and fall in bad. The report, in 1934, led to the creation of Gross Domestic Product, which became adopted by the World Bank and IMF following the Bretton Woods Conference in 1944 as the driving measure to size a country's economy. In a prescient warning in the same paper, Kuznets recognised the shortcomings of this measure, 'The welfare of a nation [...] can scarcely be inferred from a measurement of national income.' This warning went unheeded, however, and over the course of the next 70 years GDP became the main concern of heads of state, ministers of finance, central bank governors, and electoral manifestos. There was a relentless pursuit of growth, regardless of whether it was 'good growth' or 'bad.' 'It's the economy, stupid,' became the mantra for successive leaders.

Leaders were rewarded for developing offshore oil and gas fields, awarding licences to industrial fishing fleets, and constructing new hotels on fragile ecosystems rather than for making more equitable choices for future generations or restraining production to allow nature to thrive. Kuznets continued to warn about the oversimplification of his creation: 'Distinctions must be kept in mind between quantity and quality of growth, between its costs and return, and between the short and the long term. Goals for more growth should specify more growth of what and for what.'

In most market economies in the West, businesses were also expected to grow. If business leaders failed meet shareholder expectations, they could expect either to be removed or to have their businesses disrupted by the financial markets, competitors or a smarter business model or practice. With the Fourth Industrial Revolution on the doorstep, many business leaders find they cannot truly turn their attention toward more sustainable or long-term business models unless customers are demanding a price premium for such value.

Customers have also become more concerned with economic security, jobs, and affordability. As urban middle class life became more pressured and as millennials saw higher unemployment and growing inequality, some of the choices that consumers faced were seen as a luxury. When it came to purchasing higher-price, more sustainable products, only a certain category of consumer was making its choices based on the values of environmental sustainability, from which they were largely removed on a daily basis.

On the whole, our entire economic system became incentivised to focus on short-term optimisation at the expense of future generations.

There have been several attempts to shift to longer-term thinking. A wave of independent central banks were created in the 1990s with the aim of putting decision-making at arms-length from political task-masters in an attempt to end the boom-and-bust economic cycles that mirrored political cycles. Governors of such institutions were unelected but accountable to elected officials. They were responsible for pursuing long-term policies through robust and credible actions. The mandate of their decision-making committees was to meet the Government of the day's economic objectives whilst balancing economic growth (GDP) and employment, with a sense of when the system was 'overheating,' using inflation as a guide. They often had to process very complex information and use blunt tools—such as interest rates—that would work through the system over the course of two or three years. More recently, long-term capital such as pension funds, sovereign wealth funds, and reinsurance firms have seen the benefit in deploying much of their capital as share-holders and investors into investments that would de-risk the future.

Others have argued that we need to be bolder. The King of Bhutan famously called for a Gross Happiness Index, Nobel Prize winner Amartya Sen helped to create the UN's Human Development Index, and British Economist Richard Layard has explored the contradic-tions of growing economic prosperity but declining happiness in the West. For a period, the World Bank pursued an approach of Natural Capital Accounting, and the lens of the Wealth of Oceans has helped raised oceans up the agenda among certain leaders. More recently, the Governor of the Bank of England and Chair of the G20 Financial Stability Board, Mark Carney, set up a task force in 2016 setting out a framework for central banks and other lenders within the financial ecosystem to disclose their exposure to climate change. The Task Force on Climate-related Financial Disclosures (TCFD) will develop climate-related financial risk disclosures that start a process of radical transparency of the true long-term costs of climate change to companies in the G20, and inform investors, lenders, insurers, and other stakeholders. It remains to be seen whether this latest attempt can become a true system-wide reform, but the previous efforts to move beyond pure GDP have so far remained fringe experiments around which there is not yet a global consensus. Each contains its own systemic risks if pursued by only looking at narrow measures of growth, degradation, and not fully understanding the complex, dynamic enviro-socio-political-economic-system we are in.

So where do we turn?

CAN THE FOURTH INDUSTRIAL REVOLUTION CATALYSE A POSITIVE VALUES REVOLUTION?

Beyond the new industrial winners and losers of the Fourth Industrial Revolution, how can our new technologies help bring about new shifts in what we value?

Trust is an important currency of the new economy we are creating.

The new economics of the Fourth Industrial Revolution will be built around notions of trust. New forms of transactions are taking place between humans. For some, it is financial (via digital platforms of peer-to-peer lending or social currencies), for others it is social (such as sharing links or 'likes' on Facebook), for others it is bartering for services (it is estimated that over $16 billion of transactions took place on consumer-to-consumer and business-to-business platforms in the US in 2016, and similar trends are being repeated around the world).

Compared to this new world, the third industrial revolution notion of 'money' as value can seem outdated. Money is being hollowed out both as a storage of wealth and as a medium of exchange. In previous industrial revolutions, cash was a one-off, cold transaction with no memory.

Now, transactions can follow individuals around, shaping behaviour and values.

Purchasing habits, shopping history, travel patterns, and investment history can all be captured, bartered, or traded for additional services. Whether at an individual or institutional level, reputations are being shaped in new ways. For example, whereas personal investment portfolios often followed the highest returns, we can now share value preferences and ensure that not just current investments but records of all historic investments are in line with the value sets of individuals (e.g., full transparency of supply chains, low carbon assets in line with the Carbon Disclosure Project). This will have a profound impact on shifting behaviour from Stated Preferences to Revealed Preferences; if a consumer was to express a preference for organic products but consistently purchased products that were not organic, this contradiction could be discovered.

This offers new levers both to highlight individuals' planetary footprints and allocate credits to them based on what we might call 'good behaviour'. As the system of trust evolves, social marketing techniques can shape behaviour and reward actions that promote a healthy planet.

CAN WE ACHIEVE UNIVERSAL OCEAN VALUES?

At the same time, there may be biases in algorithms created and echo chambers that lock certain communities into their own 'information ghettos'. We need to be cognizant of this and find ways to identify when such biases occur in order to break through and shine a light on behaviour.

For some, like those who might rather pump raw sewage into the world's rivers or allow plastics to wash into the sea along with agricultural or industrial runoff, the new behaviours and values expected will bring a higher cost to radical transparency will force many of these industries to face greater scrutiny. It will also force behaviour change on these industries and essential infrastructure that would otherwise have stayed in the shadows.

In order to ensure a level playing field at the global level, it is also important that there is full transparency how each country is acting on the ocean. How are its citizens treating the oceans? How do its businesses treat the oceans? How effectively are its regulators governing domestic ocean waters and engaging in international ocean decision-making forums? There will be nowhere left to hide.

CODIFYING VALUES

Throughout history, new institutions have shaped our values and also codified them.

In the past, they have done this in a variety of ways. Our moral imperatives were laid out in scriptures, our religious tenets preserved in sacred texts such as the Bible, the Bhagavad Gita, the Koran, the Torah, and the Guru Granth Sahib.

As new industrial revolutions created new institutions, we started to see a range of innovations that guided behaviour. We have, of course, the Hippocratic Oath at the root of medical ethics, and our political values have also been codified in constitutions and agreements like the Magna Carta and the US Declaration of Independence (1776), the latter defining the inalienable rights of man as being 'Life, Liberty, and the Pursuit of Happiness'. We have the US Bill of Rights, ratified in 1791, which set out protections for individual liberties. The French Revolution (1789–1799) was defined by the universal values of *Liberté, Fraternité, Egalité*. We even have treaties and conventions governing how we go to war with one another

The thrid industrial revolution was marked by different moral codes ranging from The Universal Declaration of Human Rights (1948) at its beginning and the ICANN's principle of net neutrality, by which service providers treat all internet traffic similarly regardless of user, content, or website, at its end.

Throughout the 20th century and as the third industrial revolution evolved, a new ethos was needed to guide employee behaviour as large multinationals started to expand around the world with employees numbering in the tens and even hundreds of thousands. At one end of the spectrum, risk-averse firms defined employee behaviour in very detailed Employee Handbooks or Standard Operating Procedures that were hundreds of pages long. They were designed to cover every eventuality, and when the unexpected occurred, these manuals were then revised and rewritten. In many more nimble, innovative, higher-risk organisations, employees were empowered to take judgment calls based on very short guidance. 'The customer is always right' started off as a motto at Selfridges in London, and as we move into the end of the third industrial revolution, we had 'Don't be evil' from Google and 'Truth at all costs' from the world's most successful hedge fund, Bridgewater Associates.

In the era of the Fourth Industrial Revolution, the boundary between employees, community, and the customer will become increasingly blurred. We will need new forms of codifying behaviour, values, expectations, and norms.

The adherence of this can be seen through new forms of data, transactions, and footprints and can be benchmarked to others too. As the new organisations of the Fourth Industrial Revolution start to be guided by source code, kernels, and algorithms that guide behaviours, what are the algorithms of the future that should guide behaviour on our oceans?

There are advantages and disadvantages to each and every format. Some are eternal when they might benefit from being updated. Others are so open to change that they become obsolete in the face of change.

Which format would be best suited to our relationship with the ocean? How do our values translate into or usurp an economy so dedicated to production and consumption as a measure of progress? How do we incentivise industry, government, and society to adopt guiding principles and priorities that allow us to live in harmony with the ocean and our wider environment? If GDP is currently king, how do we depose it and with what do we replace it? What will our new 'oceanomics' look like and how will it work?

What guiding principle or set of principles will stand the test of time over the coming years, guiding our behaviour as we encounter unimaginable moral and ethical quandaries? How rigid should it be so as to strike the essential balance between suggestion, prescription, and proscription? Will it run to some 200 pages, like the UN Law of the Sea? Or will it be something that can be said in as much time as it takes to think it?

On the one hand we might be optimistic and design for success, articulating our aspiration for what the co-existence of humans and ocean life should look like. Perhaps this version would take the form of a 'Bill of Rights' for the ocean or a series of detailed standard operating procedures. Or perhaps it could a simple guiding framework for all activities that impact our ocean: 'Be good to our oceans as well as future generations.' At the same time, it might be wise to balance our optimism and define what we should not do. Perhaps, 'Do no harm to our oceans, nor to the opportunities for future generations.'

From these two bookends, we may then be able to derive complementary algorithms that govern our social, industrial, technological, and governmental activities.

Could this overarching directive take the form of a single, digital, master algorithm or 'Prime Directive' to guide us through the Fourth Industrial Revolution?

CHAPTER SEVEN

If I had asked people what they wanted,
they would have said faster horses.

— Henry Ford

Ocean Innovation Springboards

AS ANY ECONOMIST WILL TELL YOU, the only thing you can be sure of when you make predictions about the future is that you'll end up explaining why you were wrong.

However, the colossal and far-reaching power of the Fourth Industrial Revolution is unlikely to leave many human systems entirely intact, be they political, industrial, technical, or even moral. Our day-to-day lives will continue to change, businesses and even entire business models will rise and fall, new technologies will appear commonplace, current ones will be reconfigured or repurposed—or combined in new, extraordinary ways.

Even if we can't say precisely what the future will look like, we can and should at least try to anticipate it. Innovation, after all, is rooted in imagination.

What has the same transformative potential that steam, oil, and electricity had in the past? Which revolutionary technologies are under development that might be comparable to ship-to-ship radio or ship-to-shore satellite communications? What could be this generation's equivalent of new open water fishing fleets or deep-sea oil rigs? What, for the sake of argument, might be five infrastructures that could transform our ocean over the next quarter of a century?

Just imagine, for example, a digital ocean avatar, a highly sophisticated simulation that collates, processes and helps interpret the huge amount of data we're now able to collect. It could allow us to run simulations and help us discover potential consequences of our intended actions. More than this, though, it could operate amid the Internet of Things, perhaps helping to control fleets of autonomous ocean vessels that we use to monitor and govern ocean ecologies.

These networked, autonomous fleets wouldn't just reduce maritime accidents. Just think how they would transform global supply chains both at sea and on land, running logistics, improving performance, and optimising efficiency.

Or envisage a new generation of autonomous aquaculture that relieves pressure on wild stocks as our demands for seafood increase, and does so without the damaging environmental side effects by which the industry is currently blighted.

We might picture the possible advances in biomedical engineering that could, through genetic regeneration, aid in the recovery of damaged marine environments and restore ocean health.

Who knows what innovations in subsea robotics and smart materials we'll see? Who knows how they'll help meet our energy needs and, by extension, much of our need for fresh water, thanks to new, deep-water energy platforms that exploit ocean currents and hydrothermal vents?

None of this will happen on its own, however. It will require more than just imagination. It will require a fresh, integrated way of thinking about talent development and leadership, financial tools, policy platforms, as well as government involvement. We can, if we choose to, ensure that we nurture the kinds of business models that will secure our technological advances and, with them, our future.

The steam that powered the first industrial revolution brings to mind certain images, half-remembered paintings of fire and smoke. The oil and electricity that powered the second revolution conjures other images, perhaps sepia-tinted photographs of lightbulbs and Tesla coils, oil-powered ships, and submarines.

As the third revolution kicks off, the dawn of the microchip coincides with the dawn of colour photography and yet more images proliferate: nuclear bombs and power stations, supersonic flight and space exploration, televisions and PCs, solar panels and cell-phones. These images scroll past faster and faster, getting sharper and sharper until we get to the cutting edge of now: biotech, smartphones, 3D printing, AI, and driverless cars.

Similarly, as we look back over the past we see how business has been transformed again and again. From the archetypal industrial magnates of the 19th century through to the corporate emperors of the 20th century, from the Masters of the Universe typical of the 1980s to the young technocrats of today, we can see how business models have changed. Ownership of a resource is no longer as important as access to a service, growth is no longer defined by infrastructure, and assets aren't necessarily tangible.

As innovation has increased, costs have plummeted. Aerial drones that cost $100,000 in 2007 cost $700 six years later. 3D printing machines that cost $40,000 in 2007 were available for $100 by 2014. DNA sequencing that cost $2.7 billion in 2000, had fallen to $10 million in 2007 and $1000 by 2014. Solar panels that once cost $30 per kWh in 1984 now cost $0.16. 3D sensors used for autonomous vehicles that cost $30,000 in 2009 are now being produced for under $80. And smartphones, the ubiquitous invention in the palm of a citizen's hands that cost $499 in 2007, are now available for $10, opening up computing power greater than that which put a man on the moon to almost every citizen on the planet.

The images that the future suggests are harder to make out altogether. They form an unstructured collage of past predictions, dreams of utopia alongside dystopian nightmares. What new technologies await? What new kinds of businesses will top the indices?

Whatever our predictions, there's little we can be certain of other than that they'll almost certainly be wide of the mark. Looking to the future isn't, however, a waste of time. As the French mathematician and theoretical physicist Henri Poincare put it: 'It is far better to foresee even without certainty than not to foresee at all.'

Some innovations will pour into the ocean realm from outside; some will pour forth from the ocean and disrupt other realms. The fusion of our physical, digital, and biological systems is set to change almost every industry, disrupting some, destroying others—but creating many more. Given the speed and power of this Fourth Industrial Revolution, it's unlikely that any industrial sector or indeed any area of human endeavour will be unaffected. Energy and food production, transport, and governance are all as vulnerable to change today as they were in past revolutions. How business models change as we move away from ownership to a sharing economy, an economy in which the cost of expansion, like the cost of supply, dwindles steadily closer to zero?

What might the future hold 10, 20, or 30 years from now? How can we tell far-fetched science fiction from the merely improbable, or the probable from the merely possible?

So, with due humility as well as with all apologies due to future readers blessed with the wisdom of hindsight, we would like to suggest five possible innovation and industrial platforms that could define this new era and mankind's relationship with the ocean in particular.

1. A DIGITAL AVATAR OF OUR OCEAN

We are entering a new era of Big Data. Civilisation has produced more data in the past two years then in the previous ten thousand. The proliferation of sensors, the increase in processing power and the reduction of costs of data storage is catalysing a data revolution.

What does this mean for our oceans?

Whereas in the past we have relied on traditional marine science and sensors to collect data on our oceans, we now have a proliferation of new forms of measurement tools. These include new forms of satellite sensors—from both state-backed and private sources.

The nature of the revolution is not just about the volume of data, but also about the variety and velocity of data. We are receiving more data from differing sources at a rate that was unfathomable even five years ago.

Whilst we will build new systems to collect, integrate, process, and interpret this data, we can imagine the multitude of new Big Data applications that could be developed. We can then imagine the algorithms, deep learning, and artificial intelligence that could be applied to these data fields to train a whole new set of predictive analytics capabilities.

However, what if we truly project into the future? Whilst there may indeed be a world of competing data ecosystems, data standards, and even algorithms, we can also see the potential for pure progress.

Imagine a digital ocean avatar that would allow us to trial new activities in the ocean in the virtual world, before bringing this into the real world. As we start to become more advanced in new forms of deep-sea energy, bioengineering, dredging, drilling, and aquaculture, we may wish to model our plans in an advanced virtual simulator such as this to predict the potential impact they could have, and either make adjustments to minimise impact or, where this is not possible, ensure there are appropriate externality payments to compensate for any damage caused.

This could be more than a mere dashboard. This digital avatar could, when we deem it safe, influence the Internet of Things on the oceans and conduct Machine to Machine operations that put our plans into effect whilst employing its own prime directive quoting 'dos and don'ts', flagging suspicious behaviour, and identifying emerging trends before we pass tipping points.

This would have a profound impact, enabling us to sidestep well-intentioned but ultimately misguided plans and uncover dangerous consequences that we might otherwise overlook. It would also mean that maritime zones could be governed and regulation enforced in radically new ways, and the zones themselves could be redrawn in real time to encapsulate entire mobile biological systems rather than static Marine Protected Areas.

2. NETWORKS OF AUTONOMOUS VESSELS

We are already at the start of the self-driving vehicle revolution. The concept was pioneered by Google in 2009, and at the time of writing, there are 33 corporations working on autonomous vehicles for civilian use.

In aviation, there have been pilotless drones (or Unmanned Aerial Vehicles) since 2000. Like so many new technologies, this one was born of the military, but now they are increasingly being adapted and developed for civilian use for use in everything from filming and photography to home delivery. The pace of adoption exceeded all expectations. By 2012, the US Air Force was training more new UAV operators than fighter pilots.

At sea, we're already seeing an explosion of vessel telematics capturing data from all sorts of advanced indicators and sensors that are wired into ships from the bridge to the engine room. Furthermore, we have seen some early attempts at vessel autonomy, not just in the US Navy where we might expect to find them but also in civilian companies like Liquid Robotics and SpaceX, who use a drone ship on which they land reusable rocket boosters.

Machine-operated vessels wouldn't just reduce maritime accidents, 80% of which are caused by human error. The same systems could, with the right sensor array, limit the accidental introduction of invasive species via ballast water and reduce the possibility of whale strikes.

These machines could form entirely new categories of seagoing vessels such as remote guardians of the oceans that monitor ocean health, inform ocean governance, and, as suggested above, help regulatory authorities protect maritime areas.

They could run on new sources of renewable fuels, staying at sea for months or even years at a time. Imagine what the shape, size, and uses of vessels could be if they did not need to have people on board. Why would we need large coastal patrol boats when fleets of hundreds of low-cost autonomous marine vessels could patrol a much larger area capturing activity via video and sensors on board at a fraction of the cost? Imagine the potential for many non-OECD countries that would otherwise have to significantly invest in second and third industrial revolution technologies and invest the human capital needed to operate this.

Or imagine if autonomous vessels and robots could be designed and assigned specifically to carry out other particular tasks or respond to certain threats by, for instance, culling invasive species within designated areas, collecting plastic waste, or cleaning up oil spills.

Autonomous vessels, like driverless cars, could also improve efficiency—particularly when effectively networked. Efficiency is an excellent thing whether you're a shipping company or a salmon: Less time and fuel wasted, less noise, less unintended catch being thrown back dead into the sea.

These networks would have a transformative impact on how global supply chains are managed in terrestrial and maritime sectors. Even semi-autonomous vessels under human command could do this, as indeed they do already. We're currently seeing in every transport industry how relatively basic telemetry can improve fuel economy, speed, and scheduling. Even the smallest improvements have profound effects on a business' bottom line if scaled over time or large volumes. Given that shipping contributes 10% of all our greenhouse gas emissions, these improvements would also have a profound effect on the environment.

3. NEW MODELS OF AUTONOMOUS AQUACULTURE

We have come to rely heavily on our oceans as a source of food. Indeed, as our population approaches 10 billion, we will come to rely on them even more.

Aquaculture has been the fastest-growing source of protein in the history of the world, and in 2014 the industry hit a significant landmark when more seafood was harvested from aquaculture than from wild fisheries.

As we increase our reliance on managed resources and aquaculture rather than wild-catch fisheries for our seafood, we will need to ensure that the carrying capacity of the oceans is restored to a sustainable level. New models of autonomous aquaculture would allow us to develop seafood resources sustainably and restore our over-exploited fish stocks to healthy levels.

The industry is already developing apace, and we are currently experimenting with self-contained aquaculture systems, employing natural biological systems like bottom feeders to more closely mimic the natural environment to minimise impact. We are in some cases moving it away from the ocean altogether and onto land. Technologies such as Recirculating Aquaculture Systems (RAS) are bringing about a radical transformation, pioneering the reuse of water so as to allow for more intense growing of fish in large land-based farms.

However, the industry has had its fair share of challenges, not least among them the effects of nutrient and pesticide pollution and sea lice–related harm to wild stocks. Salmon farms in Scotland, for example, also produce around half as much raw sewage as the entire human population of that country each year.

Then there are the well-documented reports of human rights abuses among the 100 million people who work in fishing industry on vessels, transhipment, processing plants, and aquaculture farms that have been reported on in Thailand, Indonesia, the Philippines, China, and others.

Imagine, though, the potential advances that the next industrial revolution could make possible in terms of social responsibility and safer work environments.

With the low-cost sensors, machine-to-machine technologies, satellite technologies, Big Data, machine learning, and autonomous robotics, aquaculture could look radically different in the near future. Why, for example, would humans have to be involved in production when we can have a self-enclosed system that makes far greater use of natural processes and symbiotic relationships between species?

Imagine if, instead of being anchored by the coast, these farms were mobile and able to mimic the long migratory journeys of wild fish? When sensors detect the batch is ready for harvest, the entire crop could travel close to the end market.

When the car was invented, many people forecast the end of horseback riding. The activity continues, of course, but is seen as a luxury that few can afford to indulge, a far cry from its roots when horses were simply an essential form of transport. We can see the same with wild-catch fisheries, where the majority of seafood may be caught autonomously, but some nostalgic individuals will continue wild-catch practices, though perhaps not on a fully commercial basis.

As the industry matures, however it matures, we will still need better governance and regulation. We also need more innovative aquaculture techniques that can operate far from coastlines and integrate with other biological systems to ensure a healthy sea floor and balanced ecosystem. The next generation of aquaculture techniques and models could address the environmental, food safety, and social challenges of the seafood industry.

4. MARINE BIOLOGICAL ENGINEERING

As we look not just to limit the harm we do to ecosystems but also aid in their recovery, we will face huge ethical challenges alongside technological and scientific ones. Debate has been raging for some time over high-yield, genetically modified crops and fast-growing fish, for example, but far greater questions have yet to be asked, let alone answered.

Imagine if we could bring back the dodo. Should we? We killed it off, some would argue, so we should bring it back. Or the woolly mammoth? That's less easy to argue. But now that we face large-scale extinctions in the ocean, we have to ask ourselves such questions. We have to examine our values and we will almost certainly have to adjust them. We will have to ask ourselves what we're willing to do as and when more traditional forms of conservation prove ineffective.

Bioengineering's potential to open up extraordinary new avenues to restore ocean health is as great as its potential to turn our ethics inside out. The power to reproduce genetic material in the lab could free biomedical science from the need to harvest huge numbers of marine organisms to find that same material in the wild. The invention of CRISPR has given us a glimpse of what is possible when it comes to genome editing and biomedicine.

When it comes to tackling ocean health, we may soon be able to restore depleted populations that are under threat such as bluefin tuna, whales, sharks, and the world's rarest marine mammal, the vaquita.

Perhaps biotechnology that allows us to restore depleted resources or repopulate entire ocean dead zones will soon become available. We may even be able to tweak the genetic makeup of certain organisms such as coral to make them more resilient to more acidic or warmer waters.

Why shouldn't we dream a little bigger, though? What if we were able to produce biological organisms that could reduce acidity or trap carbon in some more advanced, more efficient way than we can ourselves?

Whatever our ethical objections (and they are various and valid), is there not an argument for investigating the viability of these advances anyway? If, in the future, conditions become so bad that they override these objections, would it not be wise to have the technology available and ready to deploy?

It is not just the genetic material that is valuable in the form of DNA for protein synthesis, recombinant variations, and the like. It is important to understand the expression of those genes in the physical or behavioural characteristics of an organism that have been perfected over millions of years of evolution. This is the relatively new field called biomimicry, where we can copy or emulate the manifestation of the coded genetic instructions for other applications. For example, the hydrodynamic perfection of the fast-swimming bluefin tuna is the result of particular design features that can only be understood by studying the physical animal, like the retractable pectoral fins that fit neatly into the side of the animal when not in use, reducing drag. Understanding features like this could be used to improve efficiencies in hull designs of submarines and autonomous underwater vehicles.

It's said that there are over 50 algorithms that describe how ants build colonies. Some of these algorithms are being applied in the machine world, helping guide how autonomous vehicles should operate efficiently and interact with one another. Imagine the lessons we could learn from the marine world, where 80% of the world's biomass exists in a range of different conditions. It is more important than ever to capture some of nature's incredible natural algorithms rather than eat, destroy, or lose them forever.

5. DEEP-OCEAN ENERGY PLATFORMS

Over the past three industrial revolutions, mankind has become more adept at going further and deeper into the oceans. We started with telegraph cables, then submarines, then offshore oil and gas wells, and now we are at the dawn of the age of seabed mining.

Every year that passes we are understanding more and more about operating in deep water conditions. The pressures, temperatures, and currents at depths of 3 to 4 miles make the environment as hostile and as difficult as space.

We are also discovering the potential of new forms of energy such as offshore wind, tidal, and even temperature inversions to create an entire new industry of ocean thermal energy conversion—an industry that was first conceived by Jules Verne almost 150 years ago in 1870 but considered wildly implausible at the time. In the Fourth Industrial Revolution, it's time to re-examine old hypotheses like this one.

Alongside the necessary innovations in submarine robotics, subsea systems, smart materials, 3D and even 4D printing, and logistics that will make all this possible, we'll have to learn new ways of developing and distributing on-demand, sustainable energy in these extremely high-pressure, low-temperature—or, near hydrothermal vents, extremely high-temperature—environments. We are at the dawn of a new industry, that of seabed mining. Companies and countries are rushing for licences to patches of the seabed in the high seas, and industry is developing the techniques to extract solid material from our crust and bring safely to the surface. What other exciting discoveries lie in wait as part of our underwater continental crust? Data and cloud computing centres, many of which sit at the centre of vast underwater networks of subsea cables that carry 90% of our internet traffic, are expected to consume 3% of global energy by 2030. Deep-water currents that are over 5,000 years old operate at depths of several miles depths and offer new, clean energy possibilities in harmony with our planet's natural rhythms. How will those submarine turbines work that harness the power of those chilled, deep-ocean currents and hydrothermal vents? What new ways will we find to capture the potential of waves, tides, and offshore wind to power these centres and keep them cool as they grow and grow? How can we use the sea's boundless energy to power our societies and provide the energy we need for all kind of things and even meet our planet's growing need for fresh water?

MEANWHILE, UNDER THE HOOD...

Innovations such as these, like the changes in values they provoke, will not simply ensue. They have to be actively pursued.

We can't rely solely on market forces, and where the market fails, governments must 'lean in'.

Nor can we rely on individual genius and moments of inspiration.

Our solutions and innovations will only come if we're willing to re-think and constantly revise our fundamental attitudes to basic issues.

Talent and leadership, from ground-level research the very highest levels of government, needs to be nurtured so that new skills and ways of thinking can be applied, and so that existing ones can be recombined in new, more effective ways.

We need look for the brightest and the best from all over the world and make the funds available to attract them to planet-critical roles from even the highest paid jobs in the financial and technical sectors.

Economists, financiers, and governments need to work together to develop outcome-oriented financial levers, digital currencies, and products that attract, incentivise, and sustain the necessary business models. We must also ensure that we allow these models to flourish by establishing dedicated ocean accelerators and incubators.

We also have to extend our thinking when it comes to infrastructure, asking not simply how to make ports work faster and more efficiently, for example, but asking how they could be used differently.

It's impossible to know which ideas will change the world and which will wither on the vine. Similarly, we can't know for sure which of today's technological miracles were predicted and which were self-fulfilling prophecies that would never have existed were it not for the prediction. Jules Verne imagined electric-powered submarines nearly a century before their invention and Edward Bellamy foresaw credits cards 60 years before their introduction. There's an aura, however illusory, of inevitability about these. But can we be sure that anyone would have invented the automatic, motion-sensing door if they hadn't read H.G. Wells or tried to perfect a hoverboard if they hadn't seen *Back to the Future*?

All we do know is this: Without the right environment and investment allied to imagination and an iron will, we're unlikely to triumph.

CHAPTER EIGHT

Anyone who sits on top of the largest hydrogen-oxygen-fuelled system in the world, knowing they're going to light the bottom, and doesn't get a little worried, does not fully understand the situation.

— Astronaut John Young
(after being asked if he was nervous about making the first Space Shuttle flight in 1981)

No Chance of Zero Risk

THERE ARE THREE RISKS we need to contend with. Taking no action at all, either through procrastination, analysis paralysis or apathy is the biggest of them.

The second danger is one born of fear and timidity. Even if we do act but we mobilise around the wrong topics then we do not address the threat but merely delay the day of reckoning. We exacerbate the arms race by giving more funds to the protection camp rather than alleviating the other pressures that the expectation of economic development continues to build. Indeed, having rigid, linear solutions means that we put off the day of reckoning only as far as the next crisis. And when that crisis comes, we will find ourselves trying to bring leaders together in response, reacting to it rather than heading it off.

This raises the third danger. If we succeed in mobilising for action, if we muster the courage to explore smarter, bolder non-linear solutions, is there a risk that we may inadvertently end up doing more harm than the good that we set out to do in the first place? How do we ensure we're still the ones in control of our destiny rather than allowing either nature or the system we create to dictate terms?

The stakes have never been higher. It is not just the lives of billions that are at stake in terms of the loss of their livelihoods and sources of protein, but the very conditions of life on our planet.

Doing nothing or sitting passively by is not an option. We are on the brink of crossing several irreversible tipping points. Those at the front line who depend on the oceans for their livelihoods, particularly many of the small island states, have been face to face with this risk for almost 20 years as major global coral bleaching events caused the life and colour to drain from their lagoons as local communities stood by, powerless to do anything but watch.

But how do we find the courage to develop the powerful new solutions we need without being paralysed by fear—fear of the tremendous power we would then have in our all-too-human hands? How do we set in place the right safeguards?

NON-LINEAR RISK

We are not in the regime of thinking that existing solutions can solve the challenges facing our oceans. Linear solutions (such as large marine protected areas in isolation) will not address non-linear, dynamic systems such as our oceans and the socio-economic systems that shape human behaviour.

The trouble with non-linear solutions sets is that they're unpredictable. We can't always be sure of the outcomes of these levers in dynamic systems. Particular actions may show up in some unexpected area somewhere else in the complex and dynamic enviro-economic-socio-cultural-political system. However, zero risk is not possible. Minimal risk is essential.

As we propose to take on non-linear problems with non-linear solutions, there will be collateral damage. We must be prepared for this.

It is similar to the risks cavemen faced when they first tamed fire. Fire was untried technology and a non-linear solution in a non-linear system. It kept them warm during unprotected winters and kept them safe from carnivorous predators. Success could grow rapidly, with the collection of twigs and bountiful supply of dry grass from the surrounding grassland to fuel this new technology. But at the same time, fire could quickly get out of control for these cavemen, and their ability to manage this risk rapidly run away from them.

It is precisely this dilemma we face today. We are playing with fire, but play with fire we must for, as Mark Zuckerberg has pointed out, 'In a world that's changing so quickly, the biggest risk you can take is not taking any risk.'

The challenge is instituting the right safeguards.

HOW TO BUILD A SPACESHIP TO PLUTO?

Maybe a good way to think about the risks being posed in the Fourth Industrial Revolution is through a thought experiment. Imagine we are asked to build a manned spaceship to the recently relegated planet, Pluto. Pluto lies almost 5 billion miles away from Earth, a journey that took over nine years for a NASA probe to travel.

Building such a spaceship presents several challenges, to put it mildly.

First, we would need to employ untested technology. It would have a small payload of instrumentation and guidance on top of a huge propulsion system. Small deflections on the way could lead to an outcome where it ends up being millions of miles off course. Just one unchecked error could lead to catastrophic failure.

It is clear what the mission must do—it must transport a manned crew to Pluto. At the same time, it is clear what it must not do—it must not cost the astronauts their lives in the process.

DESIGNING TO PREVENT FAILURE

Knowing the mission goal, we must first design for success. Here, we've defined success as transporting crew to Pluto, returning safely, and perhaps achieving some other, secondary scientific objectives along the way. Even with the best minds on the planet working toward this single and well-defined goal, this is still a high-risk venture. Many things could still go wrong.

So at the same time, we must design to prevent failure.

What does this mean?

Let's take the example of software development. In software development, there is one team writing millions of lines of code for new software programs. At the same time, there is often another team trying to make that code fail. It is only when the code is robust that the software is ready to ship into the market. In the context of getting safely to Pluto and back, this means examining every single procedure and asking not why it should work but how it might fail. The Apollo program allowed for a 0.1% failure rate. Given the complexity of the machinery, however, and the vast number of components involved, this seemingly insignificant fraction of one per cent still indicates that the men on top of the rockets could expect 5,000 components to fail on each mission.

So how do we design to prevent failure when it comes to designing solutions for the oceans in the era of the Fourth Industrial Revolution?

There are several categories of failure to consider.

First, these are failures we can imagine or predict based on lessons from previous industrial revolutions, what we see in other sectors, or based on science, intuition, and analytics. Second, there is the category of failure where things go so spectacularly well that they end up going spectacularly wrong. This may appear to be a contradiction but, unless we fully understand a dynamic system, successes often lead to problems manifesting themselves up in other (often unexpected) areas of a system and we end up displacing a problem to somewhere else. Then there are the 'unknown unknowns'.

Let's explore each one in turn for the oceans.

'KNOWN KNOWNS' OR IMAGINABLE FAILURES

These are failures we can imagine or predict based on lessons from previous industrial revolutions and what we are seeing in other sectors. We can imagine that the nature of these failures could be environmental, economic, social, and even political in their nature.

ENVIRONMENTAL RISKS It is clear that the more untested the technologies, the greater the risk. In previous industrial revolutions, we often use laboratories to test high-risk medicines or vaccines, or conduct risky experiments. This is a way to contain some of the higher-risk experiments to avoid catastrophic failure.

The further we engage with our oceans and the more tightly wound our relationship with it becomes, so change the very nature of the risks we encounter. Take, for example, the spread and increased intensity of aquaculture, which has now grown to over 50% of our seafood. What risk is this intensity of aquaculture creating on surrounding biology and biodiversity, or with the introduction of non-endemic species to new regions of the world? How could this type of technology be tested in safer conditions?

As we become bolder with our interventions, there may be groups that explore bio-engineering (whether for financial or environmental gain). What are some of the risks that could be unleashed with uncontrolled experiments or through uncontrolled evolution of those experiments? Whenever we have engaged too deeply with the natural or animal world, we have started to encounter diseases that jump species called zoonotic diseases. Bird and swine flu, CJD and rabies, haemorrhagic fevers like Ebola, anthrax, and bubonic plague are among the two hundred or so that we know about. What are the unknown marine zoonotic diseases that could pose a threat to humans? What, we must ask, are the 'unknowns'?

ECONOMIC RISKS: *THE PRIVATISATION OF THE COMMONS* In the US in 2010, 50% of all profits were generated by just 52 companies. Six years later, the same proportion was earned by just 28. This is leading to a privatisation of markets by large firms that dominate the economy at the expense of smaller firms.

On the ocean, where ships, rigs, and other infrastructure put the buy-in out of reach of smaller firms and poorer, non-OECD countries, the difference is even easier to see. Oil and gas prospecting, aquaculture, and shipping are, at the top table, a high-stakes game played only by those that can afford it, and it's winner take all—or nearly all.

During the third industrial revolution, we saw how many of the benefits of large investment industries such as offshore oil and gas resources often went to those with the financial resources to develop them, and the skills and tools to extract these resources. Similarly, tuna fishing is a highly complex, sophisticated, and expensive undertaking, and those with the money are the ones who profit most from this $40 billion value chain. As the process gets more complex, sophisticated, and expensive, as satellites and software play an increasingly large role, this disparity will only become starker. Many local micro, small, and medium enterprises will lose out to those that can overcome the high barriers to entry to many new industries, fuelling further resentment among many poorer coastal communities who see this as yet another resource being developed by domestic and international elites.

Some oil companies such as Saudi Aramco in Saudi Arabia, NNPC in Nigeria, Petronas in Malaysia, and Petrobras in Brazil have tried to develop local workforces and local expertise, and to institute contracts that ensure at least a proportion of the profits stay 'local'. However, by and large and over time, many of the proceeds of such resources have gone either to the international firms supplying the expertise and financial means, or to local elites who control access to the resource. How do we avoid such risks in the Fourth Industrial Revolution, where there is a privatisation of profits but a socialisation of risk? How do we avoid any new firms of the Fourth Industrial Revolution becoming 'Too Big to Fail'?

THE INEQUITY OF OCEAN RESOURCES As we go further
afield and deeper and deeper to uncover the ocean's riches—biological, renewable as well as oil, gas, and rare-earth minerals—many countries aren't even aware of their resources. Even if they were, they'd be unable to develop or buy the technology required to operate in such environments. Ocean technology is already dominated by OECD nations. The risk that this dominance will continue is high. How do we look at models such as Norway's Sovereign Wealth Fund or the model being developed by the UN's International Seabed Authority, where proceeds from the subsea industry are safeguarded for the common good of mankind, including future generations as well as those in non-OECD nations?

AUTOMATION OF JOBS The third industrial revolution had a
particularly devastating impact on jobs created by the first two industrial revolutions. Where Empire, colonies, and the growth of heavy manufacturing led to the growth of shipbuilding, merchant shipping fleets, and bustling dockyards through to the 1950s, the emergence of the container and the automation of cranes, ports, and vessels left many areas surrounding ports all over the world bleak and desolate. For the second half of the 20th century, these were often the areas with some of the highest rates of unemployment and social deprivation.

Whilst third industrial revolution technologies were an important factor in reducing low-skill, low-pay, high-risk jobs, unless there was a clear transition to new career paths, this left one or two generations of workers stranded, with local and national governments left to pick up the pieces.

A recent report by the management consulting firm, McKinsey, estimates that over half the world's job categories could be subject to automation in the Fourth Industrial Revolution, with technologies such as advanced robotics, artificial intelligence, and the Internet of Things challenging job categories one would always have assumed were safe. The challenge for leaders now and in the future is in framing the new opportunities, industries, and professions that can be created in the Fourth Industrial Revolution, and ensuring that there are as many new roles created as ones being lost.

SOCIAL RISKS: *FUTURE SHOCK* For some, the future seems like a broad, sunlit upland full of hope, profit, and promise. For others, it's a land of increasing inequality, unstable, barren, and very probably violent, too. Science fiction writer William Gibson aptly remarked that 'The future is already here—it's just not evenly distributed.'

Just as we might experience culture shock as we travel around the world, so we will experience so- called 'future shock' as we progress faster and faster in the years ahead. Many people value today's companies not by their ability to emulate past successes but by their power to disrupt their respective industries. Innovation and change have a currency and value of their own. Our progress, whether technological, ideological, or even moral, is moving at a rate that can leave us breathless and disoriented. The systems we rely on to keep us grounded and pointed in the right direction—our laws, ethics, and individual moral compasses—adjust even more slowly than we as individuals do. By the time they catch up with the changes we experience, we find ourselves hurtling off in another direction entirely.

Preparing for the future is a luxury many people are not able to afford. For many, the present is enough of a challenge. If citizens are struggling to make ends meet, moving from uncertain job to uncertain job, dealing with an ineffective state apparatus, and mired in debt, despair, and hopelessness, just getting through today is hard enough. Anyway, even if we could all spare the time to think about tomorrow under such circumstances, would we really want to, and what would we do with this knowledge? It might be looking rosy for the people designing it, inventing it, buying it, investing in it, and owning it in Silicon Valley and Wall Street, Tel Aviv, and Tokyo. Future shock might be more of a thrill to them than a shock. But for the average member of society, this exhilarating feeling isn't a bungee jump or skydive—it's a free-fall.

This social risk—this cultural shock—is related to and also a function of an economic one: inequality. It can manifest itself through the system in many ways.

SOCIAL RISKS: *LOCAL KNOWLEDGE* Just as cultures can be eroded and homogenised by globalisation, this system can cause local expertise and insights to be lost as new, more standardised processes and business models arrive and take root. What we gain in global knowledge, we may lose in local wisdom.

The new systems of the Fourth Industrial Revolution could develop protocols and norms whereby such local and indigenous knowledge and expertise, even if it does not fit neatly into the new systems being created, is somehow captured for future guidance rather than being lost with each passing generation or eroded with standardised processes created from afar.

SOCIAL RISKS: *SOCIO-POLITICAL RISK* The Fourth Industrial Revolution, like the previous revolutions, will create winners and losers. These winners and losers will have access to different levers of power and influence over the system. For example, the rapid demographic and economic growth of different regions of the world means that we are now in a more heterogeneous world, a world with a greater variety of value systems than when there were one, two, or three major poles of economic and political power. As economic prosperity has a levelling effect on the international playing field, there must be room created at the top tables not just for these emerging powers but also the value systems that they bring. Similarly, within countries there also will be winners and losers, and again each group will have access to different levers of influence.

As non-linear solutions are rolled out, we should recognise the risks inherent in the transition to a new order that will be created.

SPECTACULAR SUCCESSES LEADING TO UNINTENDED FAILURES

Next, there is the category of risk where things go so spectacularly well that they go spectacularly wrong. The story of Icarus is now legendary. He and his father, in attempting to flee Crete, were relying on a very new, untested technology: flight. There was nothing wrong with the technology, but nonetheless Icarus fell to his death having flown too high, the heat of the sun melting his waxy wings. He had, in a way, succeeded too well. The very thing designed to save him ended up killing him.

The more measured, cautious approach of his equally brave father, Daedalus, was ultimately more successful—though fewer remember his name. With the thought experiment of the mission to Pluto, we can imagine early mission successes leading to overconfidence and positive bias, both of which can lead to further dangers that are liable to reveal themselves when least expected and catch a crew unawares.

Back on Spaceship Earth, we do not need to look too far to see some of these risks.

We have long decried the devastating impact of raising cattle to meet our growing demand for protein. Large livestock farms not only lead to land degradation of our rainforests and intense water usage, but the greenhouse gases emitted are greater than that of the transport sector at over 20% of the global total.

Imagine the excitement that those on the front line must have felt when the aquaculture revolution first got underway. What was there not to like? Minimal greenhouse emissions, no deforestation and minimal freshwater water usage. This, surely, was a contribution to the world on which one look back with pride for a lifetime. The industry has rocketed to success over the past two decades, fuelled by new techniques, technologies and understandable enthusiasm. However, we can now see the devastation caused by some aquaculture as a product of its own success. New investors poured billions of dollars seeking high returns, rapidly increasing capacity before sustainability standards were in place, leading either to devastating practices, poor planning, or volumes of waste that are destroying the natural marine environments.

In the immortal words of 1980s rock band Depeche Mode, 'Everything counts in large amounts.'

'UNKNOWN UNKNOWNS'

US Secretary of Defence Donald Rumsfeld famously told the press, "There are also unknown unknowns—the ones we don't know we don't know. And if one looks through the history of our country, it is [this] category that tends to be the difficult ones."

Back to Destination Pluto. When we are travelling in a spaceship at that sort of velocity, we need a few safety valves and back-ups for when things go wrong. We know things will go wrong—we just don't know which ones. This is the only way to prepare for this category of failure.

We need several forms of design interventions as we prepare our safety valves.

First, there needs to be instrumentation to sense the current and future hotspots of change. Gauges, dials, and dashboards that tell us when the system will run away or when it will not.

Second, there need to be tight feedback loops. If the spaceship is off course, we need to know soon and we need to have the ability to course-correct. This requires having the right indicators, control mechanisms, decision-making processes, fail-safes, and retro-boosters to course-correct mid-journey.

Just as back on Earth, we have to be alive to even the smallest changes in the state of the ocean's many metrics. We will have to do so in a timely manner. There will not always be time to build a global consensus by 100% of leaders on 100% of items. Our response time must be in synch with the systems and not necessarily our arbitrary 'clock ticks' of global summits.

One important safeguard is also as much with defining what a system must do as defining what it must not do. We must design to prevent failure. It is important we give guidance on how to avoid the system leading to unintended catastrophic failure.

With potential solutions like Artificial Intelligence, for example, this brings to mind Asimov's three laws of robotics, that clearly define what a system must not do:

1. A robot may not injure a human being or, through inaction, allow a human being to come to harm.

2. A robot must obey the orders given it by human beings except where such orders would conflict with the First Law.

3. A robot must protect its own existence as long as such protection does not conflict with the First or Second Laws.

In an earlier chapter, we described a potential future scenario where algorithms may guide our actions on the oceans. What about algorithms that also prevent harm?

Third, it is about developing an outside-in perspective. Given the risk of positive bias, we need to design to integrate with outside views. We need a different frame of mind and need to be able to interrogate the adjacencies to understand how an intervention in one part of a dynamic system may not unleash runaway reactions in another part of the system. Having a view from outside the cockpit can help us get a sense of how the overall system is functioning and give us early indicators of where future risks of failure may lie.

Fourth, we need to expect failure and to design flexibility into the system. Rather than designing a rigid system, where we have a belief that everything will work, we need to ensure the system is mutable and adaptive to change. Components should be replaceable where they cease to operate effectively as part of the overall system.

We are dealing with a dynamic system, and we need to ensure we have a system that is steerable, with modularity, interoperability and tight feedback loops, rather than a large, unwieldy supertanker. We have seen analogies in the past with institutions that have been created with the right intentions, but that are subsequently unable to reach a consensus or take timely action relative to the scale and urgency of the challenge.

We need such safeguards and circuit-breakers, but at a planetary level.

THE WISDOM OF HINDSIGHT

The ocean, to the minds of our ancestors, was limitless. The values governing their use of it reflected this. Its resources, they reasoned, must also be limitless.

For example, rather than judge a New England whaler captain for his legacy, it might be more useful to see his task through his eyes. Our whaler captain was not knowingly harming the ocean and to hell with the consequences. He was doing a dangerous job that provided food and shelter for his family, employment for his crew, profits for his employers, and whale oil to light the cities that awaited him at the end of every voyage. He *knew* there would always be another whale, another pod, another whaling ground. He was not evil, he was simply incorrect. The consequences of his actions were an unknown unknown at the time. They a product of his—and his industry's—own spectacular success.

However, as the whales grew more scarce, the whalers had to go farther and farther to find the next one, the next pod, the next whaling ground. The consequences became a known unknown. Our whaling captain knew there were fewer whales and that numbers were limited— he just didn't know how limited.

The process of discovering the consequences of our actions is still underway. For example, we invented plastic just over a century ago. Cheap, easy to produce, and almost endlessly versatile, it's one of those things that quietly but undeniably changed our lives. Equally quietly, equally undeniably, most of it has ended up in the sea and by 2050 there will be, it's estimated, more plastic in the sea than fish. We have no idea what the precise consequences are for the ocean, for marine life, and for us, but we can be confident that they are far from good. The same goes for mercury, PCBs, and other forms of industrial and agricultural runoff. These too, are known unknowns.

The trick, of course, is to avoid the risks we can, and turn the unknown risks into ones that we can address as quickly as possible. Each technological advance will present its own specific moral and ethical challenges as well as its own economic and ecological conse-quences. We're aware, for example, that divers who work on oil rigs succumb to aseptic bone necrosis over time—though we're not sure precisely what causes it. As we go deeper into the ocean, will we—will the divers themselves—accept these risks as just part of the job? Or would we rather see their jobs automated if such a thing becomes possible? More to the point, would they?

DEVELOPING A VALUES-DRIVEN ATTITUDE AND A SYSTEMS-DRIVEN APPROACH

Amongst the principles that guided economic leaders during the financial crisis of 2007–8, at least one very simple, very stark idea emerged as banks teetered on the edge of collapse. The four words 'too big to fail' encapsulated much of what had happened, what was wrong with the financial system, and what needed to be done. We were aware that banks were part of the very fabric of our society and the banking system was essential. We recalled the lessons of history from the 1930s and what large-scale banking crises had led to. What we had failed to grasp was that some banks could go bust but others in effect were the system. We needed them. They *had* to be bailed out.

This provoked an understandable sense of injustice. The profits had been private but the risks, it turned out, were everyone's.

We should ask what can be done to make sure that the same doesn't happen with the ocean. Though the ocean itself cannot fail, it can and it will fail us unless we do something to prevent it. As we move from living off the 'interest' of the ocean and eat into the 'capital', what new ways can we find to assess and manage the risks—and share the benefits—accordingly?

Whichever approach we take to classifying and assessing the risks we face, we have a chance to do things differently. We are building the dashboard. We have more data than ever. We're also getting better at interpreting it. However, as we have said before, it won't be the limits of technology that dictate our future and that of the ocean—it will be our values.

So we have a choice. We can attempt to avoid the most obvious risks and take the others when they come, as we have done before and be reactive.

Or we can go out and simultaneously both design for success and design to prevent failure.

CHAPTER NINE

Think of the [Ocean Liner] Queen Mary—
the whole ship goes by and then comes the rudder.
And there's a tiny thing at the edge of the rudder
called a trim tab. It's a miniature rudder.
Just moving the little trim tab builds a low
pressure that pulls the rudder around.
Takes almost no effort at all.

— Buckminster Fuller, 1972

The Leadership Moment

Systems Acupuncture

STRESSES ARE BUILDING all around us. There are the economic demands of a society that wants more in terms of more seafood but lower cost for maintaining basic infrastructure such as pollution control measures, coastal infrastructure, sewage treatment plants, the cost of food, and the associated agricultural systems.

Greater demands are being placed on governments by the unemployed as well. Millions have found that their industries have moved on or been automated, relocated, or otherwise left behind a desolate, polluted, unemployed heartland. We have seen this happen over many generations on the oceans. The hive of activity that had existed around ports for over a hundred years suddenly disappeared with the invention of vast automated ports that were situated miles away from main population centres and employed large pieces of machinery to move the containers around. Similarly, the fishing crews of northern Europe and North America have been left in high and dry as cod fisheries were depleted.

At the same time, the pressures on environmental capital have built up. Many of our ocean ecosystems are on the brink of collapse or approaching phase-change tipping points.

Our institutions and governance frameworks are unable to cope with the speed, complexity, and scale of the challenges. Our traditional levers of change—legislation, policy development, and taxation—are proving less and less effective in this new world.

We are heading into a world of unstable equilibria, where the balance of power appears to swing wildly, depending on who has the most influence on the global agenda or which special-interest group can muster the resources to pursue their own.

There needs to be a smarter, more balanced approach to managing our oceans in a way that promotes stability.

Hence systems acupuncture, a term made famous by Professor Banny Banerjee, Director of Stanford University's ChangeLabs.

This offers ways to address specific crucial points in the system and create self-improving systems that can also help us achieve all our various objectives.

Doing the same thing over and over and expecting different results is a well-known definition of insanity. If what we think might work doesn't work, why not try something that shouldn't work but might?

Perhaps our interventions so far have been too clinical. Maybe our attempts at ocean surgery are too extreme or cause as much harm to the patient as good. Maybe we have simply been treating symptoms rather than trying to cure the disease?

Let us step back and look at the overall picture. Let us remember that our overall objective is to make the patient well again.

On the one hand, the demands we have made on the ocean have grown, are growing, and will continue to grow. At the same time, governments and international bodies are creating ever more powerful tools and more restrictive legislation to limit the damage made by our demands. Greater regulation adds value to resources, spurring businesses to find ways to get round the regulations.

The system needs fixing. We have so far assumed that this requires surgery. What, though, if the system could fix itself? What if all we had to do was find where blockages were and where the pressure points are, so to speak? What if some sort of systems acupuncture will help us identify a set of interventions that will catalyse a self-improving feedback loop?

SYSTEM LEVERS AND LEVERAGE

First we have to understand the kind of system we're dealing with. Here is a thought experiment that reflects the sorts of interventions that have been attempted in previous industrial revolutions based on our understanding of our biological and environmental systems.

A simple system could be thought of as a pendulum. It is a system where a lever (e.g., pulling back on a weight suspended by a string) can lead to a predictable outcome (i.e., the weight swinging back and forth in line with the laws of gravity and motion).

The next type of system is what is known as a complicated system. This is a system made up of simple systems, where one simple lever leads to a variety of simple systems reacting in response. An example of this would be an aeroplane, which is in essence a series of systems nested within one another. Whilst it may be challenging for someone who isn't an engineer to understand the different components and electronic systems of an aircraft from engines, radar, rudder, flaps, navigation systems, landing systems, and so on, all a pilot really needs to know about are the few levers and indicators in the cockpit that control this system of systems operate.

A complicated system such as this one is guided by pulling levers that will eventually lead to particular outcomes. The previous approach of marine policy to either ban or regulate has traditionally guided our decisions, even if regulation covers a broad range of interventions such as taxation, standards-setting, and compulsory reporting. This has often been how the economy has been run, too. We've tried pulling on levers such as whaling bans, marine protected areas, CFC bans. We've tried policy levers within the various ministries of fisheries, shipping, seabed resources, coastal resources, marine security, and finance. However, we misunderstood the nature of the system we were trying to control. Spaceship Earth is not a complicated system. Spaceship Earth is a complex system.

A complex system is one where there may not be a series of linear simple systems nested within one another. Complex systems occur where there may be non-linear relations with each body, and each actor, force, and factor has an interconnected relationship with every other actor, force, and factor depending on the state of each. The state of each and every actor and factor defines the state of each and every other factor and actor in the system, leading to an infinitesimal set of scenarios. This means that the interventions needed to influence a complex system are radically different from those that would govern a complicated system.

With oceans, the relative power of different constituents varies. Fishing, shipping, tourism, agricultural, or offshore energy interests prevail over one another. Military interests vie with those of the local community interests or the natural environment. Private sector interests might sometimes have the upper hand over NGO and public sector varies, sometimes not. The power dynamics shift. The state of one actor has an impact on every other actor. Such systems need radically new tools to influence very complicated relationships.

To date, we have been trying to address the decline of our oceans using a series of complicated levers designed to control a complicated system. They may be wonderfully complicated from an engineering, financial, political, or policy perspective, but they are based on the assumption that oceans and the socio-economic-political systems in which they lie form a complicated system that can be influenced by a series of levers that shape systems nested within one another.

They have been, in short, based on the assumption that the ocean was a complicated system rather than a complex one. The role of leaders is partly to define the reality and the context in which they and their organisations find themselves operating. However, for most of the 20th century, when we started noticing something significant was going on with our oceans, our leaders tried to address the challenge with tools best suited for a different definition of this reality and a different context.

However, the real danger in all this is while leaders are struggling for control of a misidentified reality with inadequate tools, this complex system of ours becomes a chaotic one.

A chaotic system is one in which the levers one would use in either a simple, complicated, or complex system, no longer work. They don't affect the outcome. A chaotic system would be stochastic, i.e., the interventions used would be completely independent of the behaviour of the system. A simple illustration could help bring this to life.

Imagine one is spending time in a log cabin in an isolated forest. If there is a small pan fire, where the food being cooked suddenly bursts into flames, there are a range of solutions available. You could use a bucket of water or a hosepipe. You could throw the whole pan in the dirt and extinguish it that way. Perhaps you could starve the fire of oxygen using a fire blanket.

If, however, you are in a forest and there is a large, out-of-control forest fire, these solutions are no longer suitable. The levers are ineffective and you need different solutions. You'd need to run to a car and drive out of there, phone the sheriff's department, and maybe look at cutting down trees to make a firebreak.

Our oceans are analogous. They are also non-linear. They may appear normal for many years and reveal only incremental change, then suddenly we cross a point where the system is no longer a pan fire but an out-of-control forest fire. We don't know where that point is.

The tools we must develop, then, are the ones needed to govern a complex system. As we cross planetary boundaries and wander past tipping points, we edge closer and closer to the point where no lever, however powerful, can affect the outcome and where chaos reigns on Spaceship Earth.

We have seen large-scale systems change in a variety of spheres and sectors. For example, over the years high jumpers have jumped higher and higher as new techniques were introduced, from the scissors and then the Western Roll to the Straddle and then the Fosbury Flop.

FINDING THE OCEAN'S 'TRIM TABS' AND PRESSURE POINTS

When it comes to ocean governance and the task of restoring and preserving ocean health, let us think more in these terms than we have so far. We should try to ensure that the bar can always be raised.

The question remains, though, where should we intervene? How do we decide where best to position our trim tabs? How can we create the space needed to turn the rudder and then steer the supertanker that is our current ocean governance system? Where are the system's pressure points that can help us get to a more balanced system?

Donella Meadows suggests 12 points where self-improving institutional change can be administered. They range from leadership and values to the specifics of subsidies. There are many pressure points, but some can be hard to find and some are more important than others.

If we can find these points, then there's no need to go into surgery. We can make the system self-healing.

We can introduce self-improving models and principles that allow the systems and institutions themselves to create positive feedback loops. These loops can resolve self-defeating incentives, untangle legal frameworks, and align the priorities of individuals, industry, regulators, and the ocean itself.

Aligning these priorities and creating a self-healing ocean, we need to balance different interests and stocks of capital. For example, our activities and interventions are all based on a combination of economic, financial, political, social, and natural capital. If one is prioritised over the others, this impacts the other stocks of capital. We need to balance these stocks with the right sorts of feedback loops.

The feedback loops can be introduced by any stockholder. For example, the owner of a fishing fleet will always be looking to decrease overhead costs such as fuel. A new fleet of boats with more efficient designs would be one very expensive way of doing this. Installing newer, more efficient engines to the existing fleet would be a cheaper option. The costs might still outweigh the savings, however. But sensors and processors are cheap, and software is readily available. The fleet's owner might choose to install highly sophisticated but affordable telemetry systems to their existing boats and engines that govern fuel consumption by taking into account ocean currents and prevailing winds. This not only preserves industrial capital—it does so without denting natural capital.

In the past, we've seen how some excellent interventions in other sectors have turned out to be unsustainable. They were able to redress certain imbalances by putting their thumbs on the scale; when their thumbs were removed, the imbalances returned. Take Live Aid's work to alleviate famine or GAVI's work to make vaccines more widely available. These organisations and many, many others have had to pursue their goals by trying to change the system from the outside, addressing specific problems that can, from a broader perspective, be seen as symptoms rather than causes.

In oceanographic terms, our recent policies have taken a similar approach, introducing rights-based fishing to address overfishing and controls over ballast water to reduce invasive species being introduced into different ecosystems.

Where we can identify certain problems, where the risks are known, we need a new approach to solution design.

If we look at the collapse of coral reef ecosystems, for example, we know what the problem is and we even know the causes. But we have yet to design the lever that can adjust the complex systems behind these causes—climate change, siltation, ocean acidification, local tourism, and land-based pollution.

As we have said, however, the scale of the challenge we face is something new when it comes to restoring overall ocean health. And we must take into account unknown problems with unknown causes that will require similarly unknown solutions.

We need a new, scalable form of solution and intervention design. We need systems acupuncture, and we need 'trim tabs' to create the low-pressure spaces in which leaders can come together and help move the supertanker around. It's not just a matter of recognising the tragedy of the commons. We have to find a way around or through it. We have to ensure on a practical level that collective welfare triumphs over individual self-interest.

SYSTEM LEADERS

Tomorrow's leaders, the people who are going to be administering this acupuncture, will have to fulfil the role played by orchestra conductors. Orchestras, of course, rely on excellent musicians who know their parts, but even the very best musicians need a conductor if the orchestra is going to perform. This is not a limitation of musicianship, rather a requirement of orchestration.

As such, these new leaders will also have to oversee and interpret the full score of *The Ocean Renaissance*. In the context of ocean governance, this means setting the leadership priorities, forming and preserving coalitions, holding these coalitions to account, and ensuring that the right scalable solutions are developed and implemented at the right time and the right place, and that these solutions are allowed to flourish.

These leaders, then, will need experience of leading large organisations in complex industrial (and natural) ecosystems, maintaining stability in one area of governance but fostering change in another as the situation demands.

They will need more than experience, though. They will need to think across disciplines, sectors, and industries. They may have exceptional depth of experience in one area, but that will not be so essential as an equally exceptional agility of mind. They'll need to need to be trend-spotters and researchers, adept at understanding new, complex systems quickly and interpreting different readings that use diverse metrics.

These characteristics combined with experience will come together to make them seem from the outside far more like artists than technicians.

They'll be overseeing a level of intervention with which many will be unfamiliar and with which some might well be uncomfortable. They need to find the 'trim tabs' of the oceans to create windows of change through which the entire system can then move toward a new paradigm of higher performance.

CHAPTER TEN

We are not going to be able to operate
our Spaceship Earth successfully nor for
much longer unless we see it as a whole
spaceship and our fate as common.
It has to be everybody or nobody.

— Buckminster Fuller

An Ocean Renaissance

OUR ATTEMPTS to halt the decline in ocean health, to restore it, and to ensure its future have so far relied on conventional, linear levers. As we begin to lose control of the complex system that is Spaceship Earth, these levers are no longer sufficient in a non-linear, dynamic world.

Whilst this spaceship of ours isn't yet spinning wildly out of control, the point where our controls stop working altogether is not far away.

We need to think differently. We need to look about us and see what tools and technologies we have at our disposal, and we need to see them in a new light. Perhaps they can be repurposed or redesigned. We also need to ask what new tools we can build given the new technologies of the Fourth Industrial Revolution.

If our answers so far have failed us, perhaps it's because we've been asking the wrong questions.

1. LEADERSHIP: *WHERE'S THE PILOT?!*

It's a common enough trope. The cockpit door swings open, alarms are sounding, lights are flashing, dials are spinning—but the seats are empty. That's when you remember: There are no passengers on Spaceship Earth. We are all crew.

Leadership gurus and business schools around the world can sit you down and describe the trends and forces that shape our lives, industries, and societies. They'll tell you in great detail what you need to do to catch these winds. True leadership, however, requires the courage to stand up and rebend these forces entirely. We need to shape our own future.

The last three generations of leaders have, whether by commission or omission, presided over the decline of the oceans. Their cumulative efforts have been unequal to the forces acting against the oceans. Perhaps it is for the next generation of leaders to apply their ingenuity to address the decline in novel, bolder, and more inclusive ways. But where do we look for these leaders?

Leadership is not just institutional leadership, but the ability to influence, mould, and shape the global agenda of the oceans. True leadership focuses efforts on the biggest priorities for our oceans, for the short and long term, balancing the needs of all, and mobilising resources. Leaders can look at the dials, understand the system, anticipate risks from outside the core system, and take preventive actions. However, there may not be one single leader, group of leaders, institution, or community which has the monopoly on setting this ocean agenda. Maybe it is a distributed authority with new forms of trust and moral guidance. However, it is clear that the oceans need strong leadership.

At the same time, there is also a war for talent, and Big Business and Big Government are losing out. The necessary mixture of skills is a scarce resource in the Fourth Industrial Revolution. The softer skills around creativity, entrepreneurship, and bringing very diverse fields together are going to be just as valuable as the hard ones. More and more of the best young brains are now making their own way in the world, following the entrepreneurship and startup route rather than working in staid, vertically integrated, third industrial revolution organisations. How do we come up with new incentives to attract the right talent toward oceans?

If we want scientist-leaders for our oceans, there's an urgent need to invest in new, cross-disciplinary, dynamic systems skillsets with which to equip the next generation of oceanographers, explorers, cartographers, marine biologists, and all future systems leaders. We need a new generation of Dynamic Systems Leaders, not masters of narrow specialisms. Given that the task ahead will take years to accomplish, we ought to look to the future as well as the present, engaging people from a young age to ensure a constant supply of fresh ideas and new perspectives. How can we ensure that the world has this new generation of leaders, leaders that are both decisive and unafraid to make unconventional decisions? How do we create the new ocean systems leadership academies of the future to rival the leadership training that is currently the preserve of the Ivy League, the Oxfords and Cambridges, the Grandes Écoles and the Tsinghuas of the world? What skills will they need in this Fourth Industrial Revolution world that we are about to enter?

2. INSTRUMENTATION: *HOW DO WE FLY THIS?!*

We're going to need a comprehensive control panel. We'll need dashboards, pressure indicators, altimeters, speedometers, and fuel gauges— everything we'd expect to find in order to monitor the complex system we are operating and the efficacy of our interventions. We will also need trim tabs, retro rockets, and safety valves to course correct.

Until very recently, this would have been merely wishful thinking. But we're developing more affordable, more sophisticated sensors, all the time and we're collecting more and more data. Our ability to process this data is growing commensurately.

In the world of banking and finance, independent central banks transcend political cycles and take on board a vast amount of information concerning monetary and financial stability of an economy. They guide enormously nuanced, complex decision-making processes with a longer focus than short-term political time horizons, and whilst they are immune to the whims of popularity and public opinion, they are still accountable to elected officials. They have, however, a few powerful levers that allow their monetary policy decisions to take effect, most famously the lever of interest rates. We should develop something similar, perhaps the equivalent of an independent Monetary Policy Committee for the Oceans, governing an Independent Central Bank of the Oceans.

DASHBOARDS What are the metrics we need to measure? How do we connect these dials and gauges? How do we tap into the proliferation of sensors of all shapes and sizes that are exponentially increasing our knowledge of the oceans beyond any individual's ability to fully comprehend this? What are the levers of the future that will take into account all the variables and ensure that improvements in one area don't lead to disaster elsewhere? How can we build in diagnostics so solutions can be suggested rather than having to be sought out? Just as we can teach machines to beat even our finest chess players, with machine learning and AI, our ocean governance system can be designed to be even better than we are in certain areas, providing action-oriented diagnostics and innovative solutions that would never occur to us, augmenting our abilities rather than replacing them.

INTERFACES The few square inches of real estate that make up the screen of a smartphone can be valued in the billions of dollars. The interfaces for apps such as Instagram, Snapchat, Uber, Lyft, Airbnb, and Amazon have generated significant value for these new businesses and influenced the behaviour of millions around the world. Every facet of our interaction, whether we're booking a cab, rating a service, buying a book, or renting a room, is carefully nudged and guided by the minutely considered design elements of these interfaces. What are the interfaces of the future that may be needed to guide behaviour of users and regulators of the oceans? How do we design and develop universal interfaces that can support more effective decision-making and also peer-to-peer transmission, monitoring, and engagement of the oceans, particularly in the more connected era of the Internet of Things?

AGILE A/B TESTING Some organisations are built on the premise that they have the answers. They design for success without designing to prevent failure. Nor are they particularly agile, lacking as they do tight feedback loops and interchangeable or interoperable components. In the tech world, the agile A/B approach is used. This entails rapid testing and experimentation of multiple interfaces, stimuli, and user feedback almost instantaneously. Algorithms rapidly run simultaneous randomised trials to assess how small changes can nudge purchasing and consumer behaviour.

How can we employ this design strategy in our ocean governance dashboards and interfaces? How can we trial new solutions and find ways to scale up rapidly, rather than waiting months or years for the evaluation of pilot projects or for research papers to be published?

MASTER ALGORITHMS It is not just the interfaces that guide organisations. Algorithms are worth billions of dollars and have helped many industries of the future. Google was built on its PageRank algorithm, and is now the most valuable company in the world. The algorithms used by ride-sharing firms like Uber and Lyft have helped generate billions of dollars of value for these organisations. In finance and the hedge-fund world, high-frequency traders use algorithms to replace human traders and make constantly improving choices. Complex image and sensor recognition algorithms are helping prepare us for a world of autonomous vehicles.

In a world where data and code are becoming so complex for any one person to have full mastery, what are the algorithms for the oceans that we need to develop? As we develop more sophisticated techniques to amass data on our oceans and more organisations start to be guided by semi-autonomous telematics, sensors, and algorithms, what can be done at the regulatory level to assess the robustness of these algorithms and the value choices they make? What are the master algorithms to guide for success and the safeguards that may have to override these? Who are the leaders who can design these—both algorithms that define success, as well as algorithms that prevent failure?

3. EXPONENTIAL OCEAN ORGANISATIONS: *HOW DO WE SCALE?*

Our oceans are vast, and we need to retool and build organisations that can help govern such a diversity of stakeholders, countries, issues, and actors. We have seen how businesses and industries that dominated the third industrial revolution are being disrupted by those of the Fourth. We need organisations built in the Fourth Industrial Revolution that can be nimble, agile, low-cost, and can rapidly scale. These need to be as fit for purpose in Singapore, Dubai, San Francisco, London, as they are in Lagos, Suva, Jakarta, Port Louis. We need interoperability, modularity, antennae around all aspects of the dynamic system, and the ability to scale rapidly, build new organisational muscle, and make decisions rapidly, whilst factoring in the existing decision-making infra-structures that form the legacy of preceding industrial revolutions. What are the attributes of organisations that we will need to guide us in this multi-stakeholder world enhanced by the Fourth Industrial Revolution?

Singularity University's Salim Ismail described a series of attributes that define businesses able to scale and disrupt much more quickly than third industrial revolution firms. This provides an indication of the sorts of organisational attributes we will need to govern our oceans in the Fourth Industrial Revolution.

COMMUNITY, CROWD, AND DISTRIBUTED TRUST

New forms of engagement and organisations are needed. Rather than vertically integrated organisations that are closed, with experts steeped in particular domains, what are the new ways to build and engage a community of interest? How can we create the social network of the oceans to guide change? There may be several layers to this.

First, a core community. This may be a core leadership group, or a network of networks. In tech, they would be considered a 'high-powered user group' of the oceans. This core community could include the key regulators like the ISA, UNEP, UNDP, IMO, the Arctic Council, and RFMOs. It could also include the national governments, private operators, and civil society with a stake in the oceans. Using the dashboards and gauges, this community's role would be to set the leadership agenda for the ocean and to prioritise and mobilise over particular issues as the systems indicates. This could be at a global, regional, national, or local level, depending on the systems that are used and decision-making value systems.

Second, engaging the crowd. Given the size of the oceans, it is about engaging the users and general population on the oceans. These may be both frequent users as well as the general public who have a general interest in the ocean. Social and crowd technologies can allow peer-to-peer sharing, whether on industry fishing platforms, on safety, coastal erosion, pollution watch, or even sourcing seafood. This crowd can help shape the agenda, engagement, and priorities of the core community.

The third important tool is one of Distributed Trust. In our oceans, information is often power. Where we do not have a have a top-down, central authority (as is the case with ocean governance) but peer regulators and standards watchdogs, and where trust and enforcement are a challenge, this is where new technologies can step in. Regional Fishery regulators depend on trust across national borders and companies. Let's take tuna, for example. They are pelagic fish crossing vast stretches of ocean across the jurisdictions of many countries. We need new techniques like blockchain—a distributed ledger technology developed for cryptocurrencies but also being explored by central banks—as a way to ensure decentralised authority and verify transactions being claimed by operators. This will not only enhance trust between different actors, but also ensure new value is created through such a trust-based system to value such living resources.

AUGMENTED OCEANS Three-quarters of the new impact on the oceans will come from emerging markets. In order for them to manage, they need to radically upgrade their capabilities. However, it is clear that this cannot be a linear upgrade. Even if they were to enhance staff in their ministries and provide them with the best leadership training and business education from the finest universities, it would not be enough. If it takes 12 hours to deploy a coast guard vessel from a port to the edge of an EEZ where suspected illegal fishing is taking place, we need a radical new way to enhance and augment governance of our oceans. Where the third industrial revolution augmented human bodies and the fourth will augment our minds, what are the other techniques to augment the oceans? Does this include satellite tracking, autonomous vessels and machine learning?

STAFF ON DEMAND As demands change within oceans, there is a need for organisations to scale rapidly. Rather than having large staff on call, there needs to be the ability to scale rapidly as needed. This can be both formal staff and front-line staff, co-opted from other industries, with the right safeguards in place to avoid regulatory capture. Having the appropriate interfaces to permit this can enable this scaling on demand by allowing access to a global pool of pre-vetted talent with an interest in oceans that can be despatched from region to region to offer their expertise—building capability but also improving transparency on performance and ability.

LEVERAGED ASSETS Similarly, in a world where there are multiple assets on the oceans, governments and regulators need not own them all—they just need access to them. There could be smarter ways to leverage assets that are owned by other operators, whether private operators, international bodies, or other states. Having the appropriate interfaces to permit this can help regulators scale rapidly and on-demand. For example, with the growth of shipping and luxury yachts on our seas, how can some of these also become the eyes and ears of regulators and environmentalists?

OPEN-SOURCE AND INTEROPERABLE STANDARDS

An important principle to help scale such an approach is to ensure that the pre-competitive standards are open-source and interoperable. This will enable the greatest innovation around the code, and its interoperable nature will mean it can be used by multiple operators to develop solutions. This need not necessarily be free, and a series of innovative business and revenue models may emerge. However, establishing that some of the core of the code is available in the public domain is critical to the success of ensuring this has widespread success and can scale globally.

4. INSPIRATION: *HOW DO WE WIN HEARTS AND MINDS?*

The United States doubled its territory with the Louisiana Purchase in 1803, 27 years after independence. As most of this land was unexplored, the first thing they did was to map the region. This then formed the basis for the next hundred years of industrial development. Over the course of the mapping, many new features were mapped, plants and animals discovered, and new passageways uncovered.

With both our high seas and much of our EEZs in non-OECD countries still remaining unexplored and unknown, there is an opportunity for a series of modern-day Oceanic Lewis & Clark Expeditions, run by a new set of countries. This will allow countries to understand what they have in their oceans, and rather than allow their coasts and oceans to become a dumping ground for surface runoff, they may actually discover

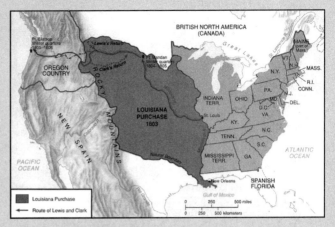

THE LOUISIANA PURCHASE
increased the territory of the
United States in 1803 by 140% or
2.1 million km2, similar to the size
of many EEZs.

SOURCE: Arrowsmith, Aaron,
1750-1823, and Samuel Lewis,
d. 1865. Philadelphia: J. Conrad,
1804. Quarter calf, boards.
Courtesy South Caroliniana Library.

THE LEWIS & CLARK EXPEDITION

In 1803, the newly independent United States consisted of just 13 former colonies in the Northeast and a population of around 4 million people. Under an agreement with the French known as the Louisiana Purchase, President Thomas Jefferson purchased the French-owned parts of America for $15 million. This added 800,000 square miles to the US, effectively doubling its size and extending its territory so that it would stretch all the way from the Canadian border and the Pacific to the Gulf of Mexico in the deep South.

Much of the new landscape was unexplored by Europeans, whose knowledge—such as it was—rested largely on hearsay. A mapping expedition was commissioned and equipped that would become known as the Lewis & Clark Expedition, after the two leaders.

For two years, 26 men traversed this new land by riverboat, foot, and horse in the company of a Lemhi Shoshone woman called Sacagawea who famously saved the expedition when she deflected an overwhelming force of Indians set on fighting by recognizing her long-lost brother among them.

They were the first team to cross the continent over the Rocky Mountains, reaching the Pacific via the great Columbia River Basin. Among their many achievements they produced 140 maps, and catalogued hundreds of plant and animal species new to Europeans such as the grizzly bear. They also made contact with 70 more Native American tribes and famously presented the President with one of their proudest discoveries—a prairie dog. Their journey would become legend, commemorated in print, in paintings and on postage stamps.

The cost of the expedition was estimated at $40,000 (approximately $125m at today's prices). The expedition laid the groundwork for the next 120 years of US industrial expansion, their maps helping pioneers plan railroads, farms, and settlements across the newly acquired territory.

the value of a living ocean and seek to protect their coasts more effectively. This could then help us understand the 95% of the ocean that has not fully been explored. This is not just about seabed mapping but also about understanding ocean currents and temperatures, and the living beings within these ecosystems and the habitats they inhabit.

As Jacques Cousteau said, people love what they understand and protect what they understand.

5. TROUBLESHOOTING: *HOW DO WE PREPARE FOR BUGS, HACKERS, AND PIRATES?*

We need to design to prevent failure. This could be unintended failure, as we discussed in chapter 8, but it could also involve addressing known unknowns and protecting the system from those that intend harm.

Since the first industrial revolution, pirates, privateers, and rival admirals in long-forgotten colonial trade wars were actors complicit in undermining a system. Two industrial revolutions later and ever since the dawn of computing there have been bugs, viruses, and piracy to contend with. We do not expect the future to be any different. Already, we've seen the vulnerabilities of many organisations to cybercrime, hacking, fake news, bugs, and biases in code, all of which are causing multi-billion-dollar damage. In whichever system we develop, we must be prepared to be nimble and to respond rapidly to the hostile threats we can expect—and those we don't see coming.

In order to do this, we need early-warning feelers, instrumentation for feedback, retro-boosters, fail-safes, circuit-breakers, and the ability to course-correct rapidly. Mutability—not rigidity—needs to be built into our system, with interchangeable, interoperable, flexible solutions that ensure we can also react in a more timely way relative to the urgency of the challenge. Let us not be naive to expect there will be those who do not seek to undermine our noble endeavour.

The defence will be a combination of the right dashboards, the right tools, the right early-warning algorithms, the crowd and social indicators, staff on demand to mobilise, rapid decision-making, safety valves, retrorockets to course-correct, and countermeasures where needed.

WHERE DO WE START?

We start where this book ends, with perhaps the most important, most pressing task of all.

We must establish a universal guiding principle that can guide our interactions with the ocean and form the basis of our approach. It will guide our algorithm, but more importantly it will define our values.

We have said that the Fourth Industrial Revolution will be guided by these values. How can we ensure that we are not left, when the dust settles, wondering how we could have allowed this or that to happen, or how we failed to anticipate the consequences of, say, artificial intelligence or biotechnology? We must start by designing for success.

The US Declaration of Independence gives us 'life, liberty, and the pursuit of happiness.' What is the equivalent for oceans? What should we take as a universal principle to help guide our decision-making? Where should we look for this moral pole star? It must be high enough in the sky to be seen by everybody, wherever they are and however high the waves. At its heart it must have a single, simple ethos, an unambiguous idea that can guide not just human behaviour but the autonomous and semi-autonomous machines we may come to rely on.

We must also design to prevent failure. Medicine has the Hippocratic Oath and, separately, the primary principle, 'First, do no harm.' There was the futuristic 'prime directive' of the famed Star Trek crew in the science fiction series about spaceships travelling to far reaches of the universe, famously going where no one has gone before. Their prime directive was to not influence any culture of more primitive nature with advanced technologies, so as not to interrupt their natural development path. As a young scientist, one of these authors was on his first expedition to Antarctica. The only rule on the boat laid down by the captain was that you were not allowed to fall overboard.

Each of these, whether fantastical fiction or humorous common sense, are simple rules. They're easy to follow and designed to reflect certain very specific priorities.

What framework, what simple set of rules should govern our behaviour in order to maintain the ocean equity that delivers a wide range of benefits to humanity? Perhaps some or all of these?

- A healthy ocean delivers vital benefits to people.

- All decisions we make and actions we take must not impinge on those benefits.

- The benefits resulting from Ocean Equity, whether they be financial, spiritual, or otherwise—are equally shared.

- We adopt the principle of Seven Generation Stewardship.

- We must restore natural capital and ensure that we live off the interest alone.

Properly developed, this charter can be embedded in our ocean ministries, encoded in our individual ocean algorithms, and adopted by the next generation, too. The values this charter enshrines will guide individual attitudes, govern corporate behaviour, and direct international policy.

Its formulation will require and encourage a new form of ocean literacy and consciousness that encompasses our scientific understanding as well as local and indigenous knowledge and social practice. It will need to bring together and balance art and culture with private enterprise and scientific enquiry. If one set of values predominates, we guarantee a continuation of the current arms race. If, on the other hand, we can amalgamate them, then we stand a chance.

As we said at the very beginning, there's no operating manual for Spaceship Earth. It's hard to believe that when he made this observation back in the 1960s Buckminster Fuller ever really thought there would be.

He did, however, leave us a clue as to how we might write one.

He had an idea for what would become known as The World Game. It was based around his contention that the world's problems had to be seen as part of one big system. He recognised that addressing them individually would never and could never work. 'Local focus hocus pocus,' he called it.

The 'game' was supposed to be played by everyone—only it wasn't a game at all. It was deadly serious. The purpose of the game was to put the players in control of the political process, forcing their governments to act according to the players' own values, to use the players' own imagination and problem-solving skills. At the time, making the game a reality was little more than a pipe dream.

Pipe dream or not, the aim of the game was simple enough to understand: *'Make the world work, for 100% of humanity, in the shortest possible time, through spontaneous cooperation, without ecological offense or the disadvantage of anyone.'*

Exhibits

GROWING SOCIO-ECONOMIC PRESSURES

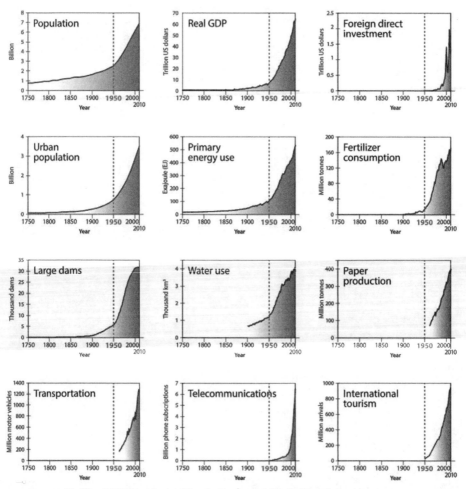

SOURCE: Steffen, Will. Broadgate, Wendy. Deutsch, Lisa. Gaffen, Owen. Ludwig, Cornelia. The Anthropocene Review. 2015. anr.sagepub.com

DRIVEN PRIMARILY BY OECD AND BRIC NATIONS

OECD   BRICS   Others

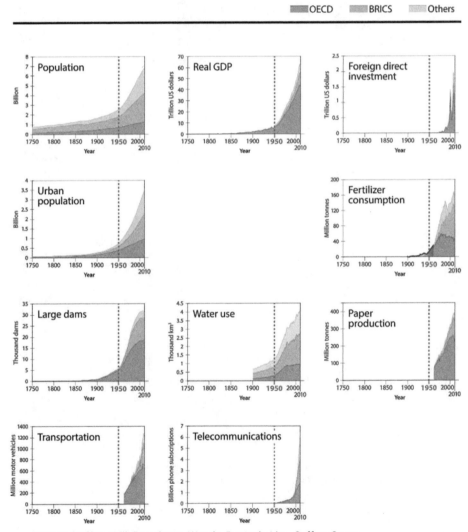

SOURCE: Steffen, Will. Broadgate, Wendy. Deutsch, Lisa. Gaffen, Owen. Ludwig, Cornelia. The Anthropocene Review. 2015. anr.sagepub.com

ARE WE PUSHING OUR COMMONS BEYOND PLANETARY BOUNDARIES AND ACROSS REGIONAL TIPPING POINTS

Earth System trends: *1750–2010*

SOURCE: Steffen, Will. Broadgate, Wendy. Deutsch, Lisa. Gaffen, Owen. Ludwig, Cornelia. *The Anthropocene Review*. 2015. anr.sagepub.com

WE ARE EXCEEDING OUR PLANETARY BOUNDARIES

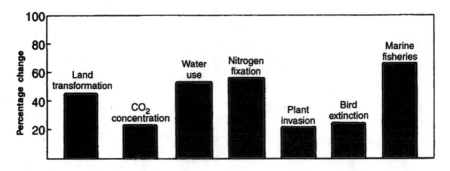

SOURCE: Vitousek, Peter M., Mooney, Harold A., Lubchenco, Jane, and Melillo, Jerry. "Human Domination of Earth's Ecosystems." *SCIENCE*, New Series, Vol. 277, No. 5325. July 25, 1997

RISING OCEAN SURFACE TEMPERATURES ARE ABOVE THE HISTORICAL AVERAGE

Global near-surface temperatures over the past 140 years

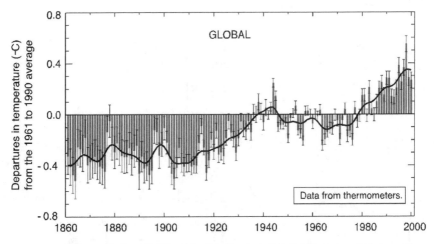

SOURCE: Brohan, P., Kennedy, J.J., Harris, I, Tett, S.F.B., Jones, P.D. *Journal of Geophysical Research*, Vol. III, D12106, October 29, 2006.

PREVIOUS INDUSTRIAL REVOLUTIONS HAVE ALLOWED US TO BECOME MORE EXTRACTIVE OF OCEAN RESOURCES...

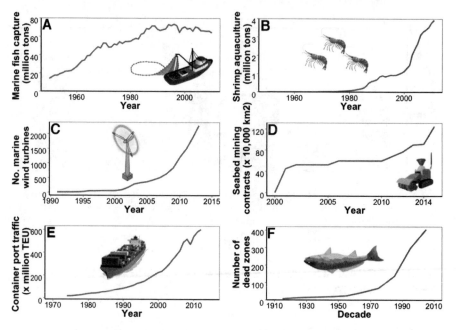

...AND HAVE A SIGNIFICANT IMPACT ON THE HEALTH OF OCEAN ECOSYSTEMS

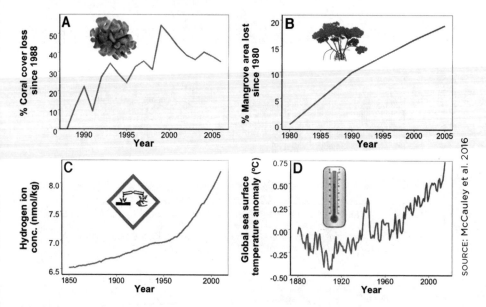

SOURCE: McCauley et al. 2016

GLOBAL FISHERIES ARE AT MAXIMUM CAPACITY, WITH OVER HALF HAVING BEEN OVEREXPLOITED OR COLLAPSED

The condition of the world's fisheries has declined drastically because of overfishing.

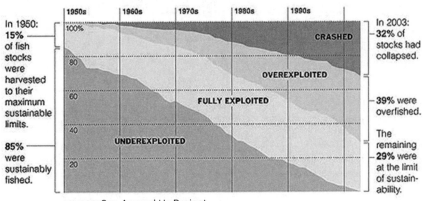

SOURCE: Sea Around Us Project

NON-LINEAR NATURE OF OCEAN ECOSYSTEMS
EXAMPLE: Cod Fisheries in the North Atlantic (Grand Banks)

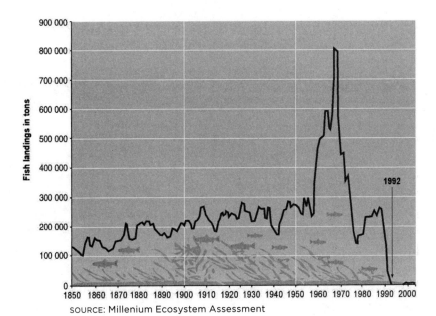

SOURCE: Millenium Ecosystem Assessment

ATMOSPHERIC CARBON DIOXIDE IS THE MAIN DRIVER OF MORE ACIDIC OCEANS

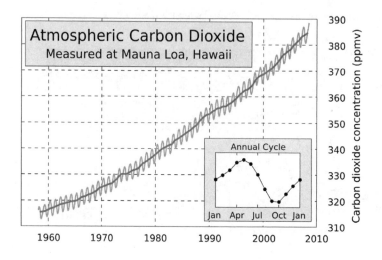

GROWTH OF DEMAND IN FISHERIES AND AQUACULTURE IS PRIMARILY BEING DRIVEN BY GROWTH IN ASIA

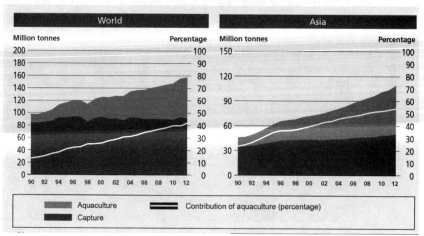

SOURCE: FAO

THE ECONOMIC RISE OF ASIA IS UNPRECEDENTED IN ITS SPEED AND SCALE

Evolution of the earth's economic center of gravity[1]
AD 1 to 2025

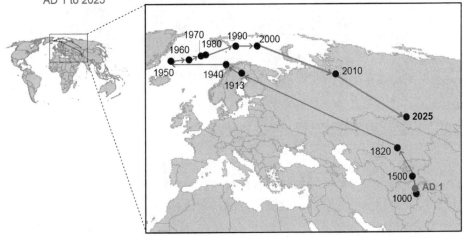

Calculated by weighting national GDP by each nation's geographic centre of gravity; a line drawn from the centre of the earth through the economic centre of gravity locates it on the earth's surface. For detailed analysis, see Richard Dobbs et al., Urban World: Cities and the Rise of the Consuming Class, McKinsey Global Institute (2012). SOURCE: University of Groningen; McKinsey Global Institute analysis of data compiled by Angus Maddison.

THE SHARE OF LABOUR IN AGRICULTURE HAS FALLEN FROM 40 PERCENT IN 1900 TO LESS THAN 2 PERCENT TODAY

Distribution of labor share by sector in the United States, 1840–2010

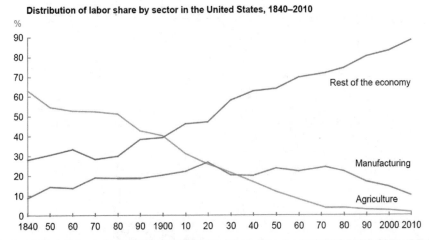

SOURCE: Stanley Lebergott, "Labor force and employment 1800–1960," in *Output, employment, and productivity in the United States after 1800*, Dorothy S. Brady, ed., NBER, 1966; World Data Bank, World Bank Group; FRED: Economic Research, Federal Reserve Bank of St. Louis; Mack Ott, "The growing share of services in the US economy—degeneration or evolution?" *Federal Reserve Bank of St. Louis Review*, June/July 1987; McKinsey Global Institute analysis

Ocean Doctrines

Leadership approaches toward our oceans over past 80 years   *Selected Examples*

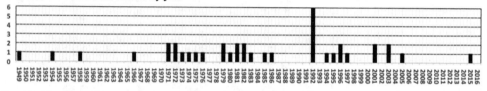

International Ocean Conventions by year

Source: Degnarain and Stone (2017)

THE CURRENT GLOBAL GOVERNANCE SYSTEM
THAT COVERS OUR OCEANS

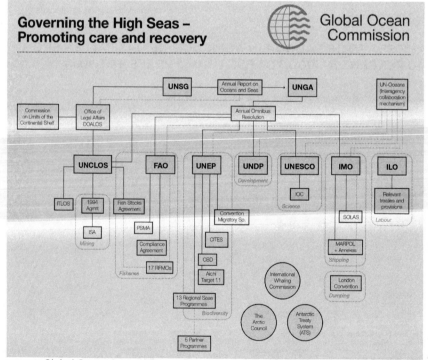

SOURCE: Global Ocean Commission

TECHNOLOGY ADOPTION HAS BEEN ACCELERATING OVER THE PAST 100 YEARS

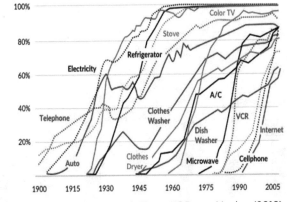

Consumption Spreads Faster Today

Percent of US Households

SOURCE: Michael Felton, *The New York Times*, HBR.org, Meeker (2016)

THE DISRUPTIVE POTENTIAL OF TECHNOLOGY IS SET TO CONTINUE WITH FOURTH INDUSTRIAL REVOLUTION TECHNOLOGIES

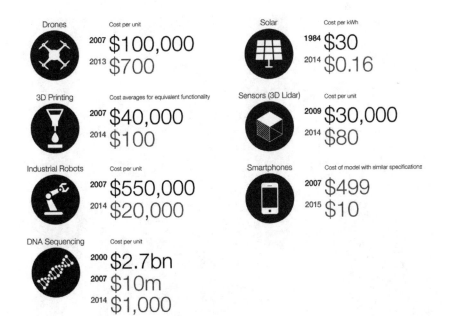

Drones — Cost per unit
2007 $100,000
2013 $700

Solar — Cost per kWh
1984 $30
2014 $0.16

3D Printing — Cost averages for equivalent functionality
2007 $40,000
2014 $100

Sensors (3D Lidar) — Cost per unit
2009 $30,000
2014 $80

Industrial Robots — Cost per unit
2007 $550,000
2014 $20,000

Smartphones — Cost of model with similar specifications
2007 $499
2015 $10

DNA Sequencing — Cost per unit
2000 $2.7bn
2007 $10m
2014 $1,000

SOURCE: World Economic Forum, Accenture, Ismail (2014)

Time to reach a valuation of US $1 billion or more
Years from founding

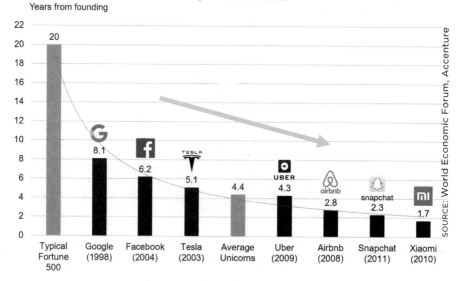

SOURCE: World Economic Forum, Accenture

MEGA-TRENDS AND NEW ACTIVITIES ARE IMPACTING OUR OCEANS

SOURCE: WEF Global Agenda Council on Oceans, Ink Strategy

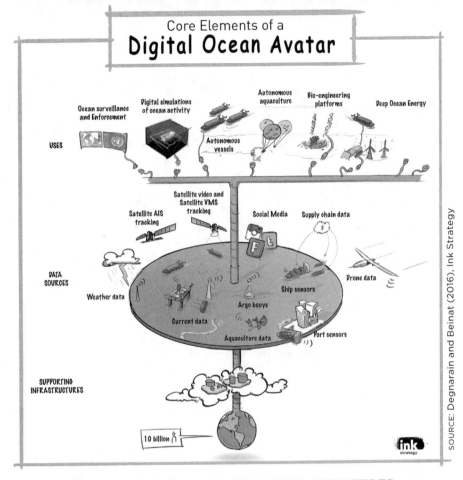

SOURCE: Degnarain and Beinat (2016), Ink Strategy

NEW OCEAN GOVERNANCE INSTRUMENTS ARE NEEDED, LIKE THE PROPOSED OCEAN ACCOUNTABILITY BOARD

SOURCE: WEF Global Agenda Council on Oceans, Ink Strategy

25 Ocean Tipping Points

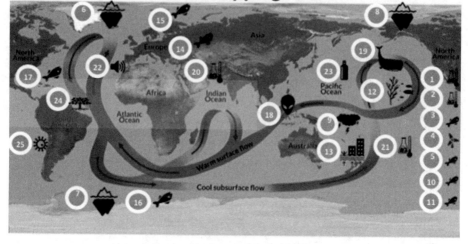

Tipping Point	How at risk are we?

Deoxygenation of the oceans

Ocean biology generates half the planet's oxygen. However, for every degree of ocean warming, oxygen concentration declines by approx 2%. Over the past 50 years, oxygen concentration in ocean water has decreased 2% due to higher temperatures. The trend is toward 3-6% decline in oxygen concentration by end of the 21st century. This will cause layers of the ocean to stratify so that oxygen-rich surface waters become less able to mix with oxygen-poor deeper waters, increasing the metabolism of marine species and increasing their need for oxygen.

Increase in ocean acidification

Ocean are the largest carbon sink on the planet, with over 90% of carbon stored in algae, vegetation and coral under the sea, and absorbing 30% of CO_2 each year. However, increased atmospheric CO_2 dissolves in seawater and makes oceans more acidic. Oceans are already 30% more acidic, especially in high latitudes. Many planktonic communities have calcium carbonate structures. CO_2 is harmful to these communities and could result in massive ecosystem collapse because food webs are sustained by plankton.

Decrease in Plankton

Phytoplankton population has declined by 40% since 1950. Plankton are the base of the food chain, with implications for the carbon cycle and marine food web. Plankton are responsible for generating half the world's oxygen and absorbing 30% of the world's CO_2. Scientists believe warming surface temperatures are to blame.

Disrupted Thermohaline Circulation

The Gulf Stream has already slowed 30% over past 30 years because of temperature and salinity fluxes, which are intensified by 'cul-de-sac' effect of North Atlantic Ocean. The Gulf Stream is responsible for the moderate temperature in Europe, without it, Northern Europe will experience weather conditions similar to Alaska. It is also possible that convective sinking of water rimming Antarctica could also change, but that system is open to all oceans via the Antarctic circumpolar current, so the effect will not be as intensified as in North Atlantic's 'cul-de-sac.'

Increase in Global Marine Extinctions

15 marine animals have gone extinct due to human pressure, and there is risk on many more. Large marine animals are particularly at risk with new risk of massive extinction wave. Already, the following have passed tipping points or their populations have collapsed: Tuna - Atlantic Ocean; Sharks - globally; Large Rays - tropics; Whales - everywhere; Turtles - tropics and subtropics in all urbanised coastal areas; Deep Sea fish - Southern Ocean, Tasman Sea, Southern Indian Ocean; Krill - Southern Ocean.

Glacial Ice Melt (Greenland)

Melting rates in Greenland have doubled since the 1990s (twice the rate of that of Antarctica), driven by a warming atmosphere and increased direct sunlight. Greenland meltwater accounts for one third of all sea-level rise. There are 660,000 cubic miles of glacial ice on Greenland, the second largest body of ice after Antarctica. If all the ice melts, it would raise global sea level by over 20 feet. Furthermore, because the Atlantic is a relatively small ocean, almost a 'cul-de-sac' pointing North, the introduction of that much freshwater could disrupt the thermohaline circulation including the Gulf Stream, impacting the weather of Northern Europe.

Glacial Ice Melt (West Antarctica)

Whilst melting rates in Antarctica have increased significantly, the heat absorbed by the deep Southern Ocean around Antarctica could lead to a significant ocean and climate tipping point. The Antarctic icecap is up to 9,000 feet thick, contains 70 percent of the world's surface freshwater and more than 90% of around's freshwater ice. A 10% portion of this icecap, the West Antarctic Ice Sheet (WAIS) is just smaller than the Greenland icecap, at 530,000 cubic miles. It is also melting, but from a combination of warmer air and warming of the deep Southern Ocean (SO). The SO circulation is driven by the Antarctic Circumpolar Current (ACC), which is the only connection between the Indian, Pacific and Atlantic oceans. While the temperature increases are small in the deep SO (about 0.03°C per decade), the huge volume of water there means that this warming accounts for a huge amount of energy storage. This is fundamentally different than Greenland where melting is primarily driven by a warming atmosphere. If this deep SO heating was going into the atmosphere instead, it would be warming at a rate of about 3°C per decade, instead of 0.03°C. As this constantly warming water swirls around Antarctica it translates heat to the ice and melts it. Another major non-linear risk is that at any moment, the WAIS could experience a rapid acceleration in melting. Given the slope of the Antarctic continent and way the ice sheets rest on the continent, melt may reach a point where the ice sheets just slide into the ocean causing rapid rise in sea levels. This kind of event could change sea level rise from being measured in millimeters per year to centimeters or even meters per year. If the entire WAIS were to melt or slide into the ocean, global sea levels would rise by over 15 feet.

Artic Melting Sea Ice

Arctic sea ice has been decreasing by 13% every ten years, and is expected to approach ice-free summers by 2025, for the first time in 100,000 years. This will create a reinforcing feedback loop, making the Earth warmer due to decreased albedo effect (cooling from sun's reflection off the white ice surface). Melting sea ice will also alter the planet's thermohaline circulation and disrupt marine ecosystems as well as negatively impacting polar bears, seals and other wildlife. Whilst some fisheries benefit from short term increase of phytoplankton from more sunlight, the loss of ice will eventually lead to a collapse of the biological ecosystem around the edge of the Arctic Ice.

More intense storms

The power and duration of hurricanes, typhoons, and destructive storms generated over the tropical ocean may have increased up to 50% since the 1970s. The strength of these storms is correlated to warming oceans and the energy added to weather systems, and are estimated to increase by 5 percent for every 1°C rise in sea surface temperature. Changing ocean surface temperatures is causing more erratic weather patterns all over the planet, over the oceans as well as over land.

Overfishing

We are taking too much complex protein from our oceans, before stocks have the chance to recover. Globally, it is estimated that 80% of all commercial fisheries have either collapsed, are over-exploited or inefficiently managed to not produce maximum benefits. Only the remaining 20% are well managed. Some species such as bluefin tuna which can live to 20-50 years, have seen populations collapse by over 90% in the past 40 years and will take decades to fully recover.

Pole-ward migration of Fish

Fish populations are moving toward cooler waters of the poles as sea temperatures rise. It is estimated the migration is almost 10 miles pole-ward every 10 years, given temperature rise forecasts. The tropics will end up losing out.

Coral Reef Extinction

Corals are home to 25% of all known marine life, and have more biological diversity than the rainforest. We have already lost 30% of the world's coral reefs, with 60% expected to be destroyed over the next 30 years based on current trajectories of warming, acidification, overfishing and coastal development. By 2050, 90% of all reefs will be threatened with extinction. Increased atmospheric CO_2 dissolves in seawater and makes oceans more acidic. Oceans are already 30% more acidic, especially in high latitudes. Coral, already stressed by warming, overfishing, coastal development will suffer from higher acidification, impacting all tropical regions around the world.

Submerged nations

The current rate of sea level rise is about 3 millimeters per year from melting glacial ice and thermal expansion. By the end of the 21st century, global sea levels will likely rise by 1-3 meters. Island nations with an average elevation of around 3 meters above today's sea level (Kiribati, Maldives, Marshall Islands, Tuvalu, the New Zealand territory of Tokelau) will be unlivable due to submergence and or "over wash" from storms, unless radical adaptation strategies are developed and deployed. These "front-line" nations have formed the Coalition of Low Lying Atoll Nations on Climate Change (CANCC) in response to this impending, existential, slow motion disaster. It is estimated over 500,000 will be displaced without a nation within two generations, and globally one billion will be displaced from low lying coastal regions such as Bangladesh, Florida, Jakarta, Lagos, and will need to move inland.

Black Sea ecosystem collapse

The Black Sea ecosystem was transformed through fisheries collapse (over 60 million tonnes of marine life lost), pollution, coastal habitat destruction. Shows what happens in semi-enclosed sea with large human populations along shore (80 million around Black Sea). The effects were intensified due to closed nature of system.

Baltic Sea ecosystem collapse

Cod population is one half its 1970s size. And the region suffers from eutrophication resulting from 78% of the overall nitrogen and 95% of the overall phosphorus coming from land pollution, mainly agriculture.

Antarctic Krill collapse

Krill is the fundamental basis of the Antarctic food web. Over-harvesting is now an emerging issue when 2010 marked the first time a krill fishery had to be closed due to exceeding the catch limits.

Growing Ocean Dead Zones

Ocean deadzones have doubled in frequency every ten years since the 1960s, particularly around river estuaries. This has been driven by agricultural and industrial run off causing "dead zones" from eutrophication (excessive nutrients and lack of oxygen). Climate change will likely worsen dead zones around the world, particularly off coasts of SE Asia, China, India, Baltic Sea, West Coast of US, New Zealand, Brazil.

Rise of invasive species

Human induced invasive species is primarily from ballast water and hobby aquarists discharging animals to wild. Disrupts ecosystems. As marine ecosystems change, there will be other drivers of invasive species, dramatically altering the biological food chains.

Iconic species collapse

Humans have conducted systematic serial depletion of ground fish, deep sea fish, whales, sharks, tuna, ranging from 30%-90% original stock sizes.

Arabian Sea Salinity

Desalination from surrounding megacities has significantly increased the salinity of the Arabian Gulf, impacting carbon absorption and marine life. High salinity ocean water is driven by growing population and water consumption by major cities surrounding Gulf, and will be further intensified with climate change increasing temperatures and water-stressed regions.

El Nino amplitude increase

Oscillations and associated ocean water heating has risen each decade, and is predicted to double in frequency with climate change. Has global impact on weather and ocean temperatures, including increased coral bleaching.

Sound Pollution

Global shipping has increased four-fold in past 20 years, dramatically increasing noise pollution along major shipping routes. Sound from seismic surveys in the Arctic is increasing due to melting sea ice and expanded oil fields. Causes damage to marine life. Also, military low frequency sonar tests kill marine mammals. Do not know how damaging or extensive, but worrying trend.

Growth of plastics

There are over 5 trillion pieces of plastic trash in oceans, increasing by 8 million tons/year, or 20 fo over the past 50 years and expected to double in next 20 years. By 2025, the ocean could contain one ton of plastic for every three tons of fish, and more plastics than fish by 2050. Plastic also degrading to "mico-plastic" becoming incorporated in living tissue. Plastic pollution driven by sever major countries: China, India, Sri Lanka, Indonesia, the Philippines, Thailand, and Vietnam.

Coastal Mangrove Forests collapse

Coastal development has destroyed or degraded over 60% of the worlds mangroves forests including from aquaculture, tourism, and general urbanization of coastlines. We destroy roughly 1 percent of the world's mangroves each year. If this rate of loss continues, all unprotected mangroves could be lost in the next 100 years.

Harmful Algal Blooms

Scientists have observed an increase in the frequency, severity and geographic distribution of Harmful Algal Blooms worldwide. Recent research suggests that the impacts of climate change may promote the growth and dominance of harmful algal blooms through a variety of mechanisms including warmer water temperatures (above 70F), changes in salinity, increases in atmospheric carbon dioxide concentrations, rising sea levels that create new shallow areas where blooms can more easily occur. Harmful algal blooms are dangerous, producing toxins that can kill marine organisms, taint shellfish, cause skin irritations, and even foul the air. These can be associated with dead zones. In the last two years, the world's second largest exporter of salmon, Chile, lost 20% of its farmed salmon (valued at over $1bn) due to toxic algal blooms.

SOURCE: Stone and Degnarain (2017)

Ocean States

Oceans as a % of Total Sovereign Area

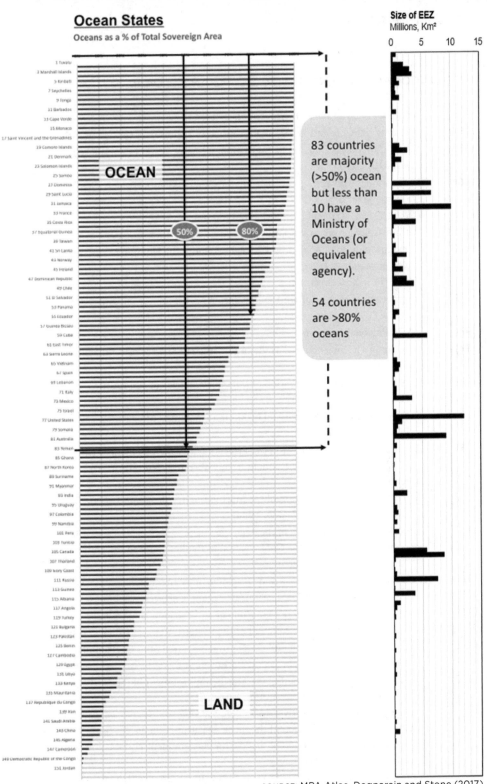

OCEAN

83 countries are majority (>50%) ocean but less than 10 have a Ministry of Oceans (or equivalent agency).

54 countries are >80% oceans

50%   80%

LAND

SOURCE: MPA Atlas, Degnarain and Stone (2017)

INTERNATIONAL CONVENTIONS: *REGIONAL AND GLOBAL*

1949   Inter-American Tropical Tuna Commission (IATTC)

1954   International Convention for the Prevention of Pollution of the Sea by Oil

1958   Convention on Fishing and Conservation of Living Resources of the High
Seas (CFCLR)

1966   International Convention for the Conservation of Atlantic Tunas (ICCAT),
Rio de Janeiro

1971   UNESCO The Man and the Biosphere Programme (MAB)
Ramsar Convention on Wetlands

1972   Convention on the Prevention of Marine Pollution by Dumping Wastes and
Other Matter
World Heritage Convention

1973   International Convention for the Prevention of Pollution from Ships
(MARPOL)

1974   UNEP Regional Seas Programme

1975   Convention on International Trade in Endangered Species of Wild Fauna
and Flora

1979   Convention on the Conservation of Migratory Species of Wild Animals
(CMS), Bonn

1980   Convention for the Conservation of Antarctic Marine Living Resources
(CCAMLR), Canberra

1981   Convention for Co-operation in the Protection and Development of the
Marine and Coastal Environment of the West and Central African
Region, Abidjan
Convention for the Protection of the Marine Environment and Coastal
Area of the South-east Pacific, Lima

1982   UN Convention on the Law of the Sea (UNCLOS)
Regional Convention for the Conservation of the Red Sea and the Gulf of
Aden Environment, Jeddah

1983   Convention for the Protection and Development of the Marine
Environment of the Wider Caribbean Region, Cartagena de Indias

1985   Convention of the Protection, Management and Development of the
Marine and Coastal Environment of the Eastern African Region, Nairobi

1986   Convention for the Protection of the Natural Resources and Environment
of the South Pacific Region, (SPREP Convention) Nouméa

1992   Convention for the Protection of the Marine Environment of the North-
east Atlantic (OSPAR Convention), Paris
Convention on Biological Diversity (CBD), Nairobi
Convention on the Protection of the Black Sea against Pollution, Bucharest
Convention on the Protection of the Marine Environment of the Baltic Sea
Area, Helsinki Convention
United Nations Framework Convention on Climate Change (UNFCCC)

Agreement on the Conservation of Small Cetaceans of the Baltic, North East Atlantic, Irish and North Seas (ASCOBANS), New York

1994   Commission for the Conservation of Southern Bluefin Tuna (CCSBT) formed

1995   UNEP Global Programme of Action for the Protection of the Marine Environment from Land-based Activities (GPA)

1996   Agreement on the Conservation of Cetaceans in the Black Sea, Mediterranean Sea and contiguous Atlantic area (ACCOBAMS), Monaco

1997   Kyoto Protocol

2001   Agreement on the Conservation of Albatrosses and Petrels
Stockholm Convention on Persistent Organic Pollutants

2003   Framework Convention for the Protection of the Marine Environment of the Caspian Sea
Putrajaya Declaration of Regional Cooperation for the Sustainable Development of the Seas of East Asia, Malaysia

2005   Western and Central Pacific Fisheries Commission

2015   Paris Agreement on Climate Change

SHARK SANCTUARIES

1980   Israel

2001   Congo-Brazzaville

2005   Cook Islands

2006   Egypt Red Sea

2008   British Virgin Islands

2009   Palau

2010   Raja Ampat • Maldives

2011   Bahamas • Honduras • Marshall Islands • Tokelau

2012   French Polynesia • American Samoa • Venezuela

2013   Brunei • New Caledonia

2014   Federated States of Micronesia

2015   Antongil Bay • Yarari • Northern Marianas Islands and Guam

2016   Cayman Islands • Sint Maarten • Kiribati

Pending   Semporna

MANTA RAY SANCTUARIES

1995   Maldives

2003   Philippines

2007   Mexico

2010   Hawaii • Ecuador

2014   Indonesia

2015   Peru

Epilogue

GREG, A MARINE BIOLOGIST FROM NEW ENGLAND, AND NISHAN, AN ECONOMIST FROM MAURITIUS, met at a World Economic Forum meeting in Dubai. While their backgrounds and specialisms were different, their passion was the same: the ocean.

Greg was born in Boston. His family tree is typical of many planted by 17th-century European immigrants to America, its branches holding an accountant, a nurse, farmers, an undertaker, a doctor, revolutionary and civil war soldiers, a buffalo hunter, a banker, and a sheriff. Greg was the first oceanographer in the family and discovered the ocean as a child watching Jacques Cousteau and *Sea Hunt* on a TV that had three networks and a clicky channel changer dial. He was fascinated by footage of SCUBA dives and shipwrecks, majestic whales, mysterious fish, and a team of French divers living underwater in a habitat drinking wine. Then, when he was seven or eight, he went to visit a cousin who lived near a beach south of Boston. The cool Atlantic and the colourful array of animals he saw underwater awoke something in him that never went back to sleep. He has spent his life diving in the ocean with everything from SCUBA, to submarines, to underwater habitats, always learning about it, learning from it, and teaching others what he has learned.

Nishan quite literally fell into the oceans as a child. He remembers playing on the beaches of Mauritius, which were full of life, colour, and happiness. His family had been entwined with the small island nation in the Indian Ocean for over 150 years. With academic training at Cambridge and Harvard and then a wide-ranging career starting with BBC, and moving through McKinsey, 10 Downing Street, Dubai, the World Bank, and then Mauritius, Nishan has spent time understanding at close quarters leadership, power dynamics, and forces that shape our economies, societies, and environment. Through leadership of

WEF's Ocean work with Greg, he has built an intimate understanding of the circuitry of global, regional, and national organisations shaping our ocean's agenda, having had a front-row seat in small island states, large countries, big businesses, and small tech startups. It is his firm belief that the Fourth Industrial Revolution will shape our societies and offers the best chance of a brighter future.

The idea for a book came from a discussion Greg had with President of the UN General Assembly, His Excellency Peter Thomson, who suggested that the 2017 UN Sustainable Development ocean meeting could be an opportunity to launch something inspiring and fresh. Originally, Greg had in mind a book about the historical relationship between humanity and the ocean. It would be part anthropology, part ocean science.

Then Nishan suggested that such a book should look forward as well as back. It should, he suggested, be rooted in the present. As the Fourth Industrial Revolution dawns, what could be a better time to take the lessons of the past, apply the latest thinking of the present, and try to establish some guidelines that might ensure a better future?

Greg started from the beginning and Nishan from the end. They met somewhere in the middle and, like two travellers meeting in some out-of-the-way spot, swapped accounts of the things they had discovered along the way.

Acknowledgments

WE ARE GRATEFUL to the World Economic Forum, Chairman Klaus Schwab, and Dominic Waughray for the time, partnership and intellectual space to think about oceans whether in the cold and invigorating air swirling around the snow-capped peaks of Davos, or in the heat of Dubai and Abu Dhabi. We thank Dan Sten Olsson of Stena AB and Suzanne and Ric Kayne, for their generosity, passion, and making it possible to complete this book in time for the 2017 UN Sustainable Development Goal 14 conference and to issue a copy to each attendee and head of state who attends this landmark meeting.

A great many thanks to President Peter Thomson for his unique global ocean leadership and belief in this book from the moment the idea was mentioned. This book reflects the contributions and support of multiple organisations including the World Economic Forum, Conservation International, WWF, the United Nations Office of the President of the General Assembly, Benioff Oceans Initiative, Prince Albert II of Monaco Foundation.

Thanks also to, HSH Prince Albert II, HE Bernard Fautrier, Oliver Wenden, Minister Isabella Lövin, Minister Teuau Toatu, Minister Tebao Awerika, Tomas Anker Christensen, Brian Skerry, Glenn and April Bucksbaum, Dianna Cohen, Harrison Ford, Ray Dalio, Peter Seligmann, Russ Mittermier, Ted Waitt, Andy Karsner, Doug McCauley, and Claes Berglund. To members of the World Economic Forum's Global Agenda Councils over the past few years for giving us your trust. Michael Lodge, Grahaeme Henderson, Juergen Matern, John Tanzer, Karen Sack, Celine Cousteau, Enric Sala, David Schorr, Pawan Patil, Jim Leape, Maria Damanaki, Justin Mundy, Tony Haymet, Michael Johnston, Paul Bunje, Anisa Costa, Amina Mohammed, Ngaire Woods, Naoko Ishii, Angus Friday, Lewis Pugh, Euro Beinat and Larry Madin. To GAC co-chair, Kenneth MacLeod for his ever present and wise counsel. We owe a debt to Steve Katona and Jared Diamond, who gave feedback on an early version of the manuscript.

I (Greg) thank Christine Zinnemann for showing me the way to the Pacific Islands and then drawing lessons, the "Sacagawea" of the Pacific Oceanscape.

Thank you President Taneti Maamau for the honor of being science advisor to Kiribati enabling me to learn so much. Thanks also to Alan and Lisa Dynner, Wendy Benchley and John Jeppson, Edna and Wendy Tucker, Ed Schiene, Sara and Frank Nichols, Gordon Moore, Beau Wrigley, Ambassador Makurita Barro, President Anote Tong, and the wonderful memories of my dear ocean friends of so many years, Teddy Tucker and Peter Benchley, who have already made port.

I (Nishan) am grateful to those who helped maintain the strong link to our small island and ancestral home of Mauritius, and for allowing me to help in some small way to contribute toward the country's future. Former Minister of Finance, Xavier-Luc Duval, for continuing to believe in and champion Mauritius in the Indian Ocean and on the global stage. McKinsey's Dominic Barton for all his encouragement to work on the biggest issues affecting this current generation of leaders. To WEF GAC Manager, Nathalie Chalmers, for giving her all for the ocean. Discussions with Global Ocean Commissions, Pascal Lamy, Trevor Manuel, David Miliband, Jose Maria Figures, Oby Ezekwesili, for their wisdom on how to build 'self-improving systems' across the global system. We are grateful for discussions with Dr Banny Banerjee over the summer of 2016 at Stanford University around self-improving systems change and Systems Acupuncture. Finally, our heartfelt thanks to Marc and Lynne Benioff for their leadership, passion and generosity in allowing us the opportunity to pursue the oceans, Doug McCauley, and WEF's Young Global Leaders and Global Shapers Communities who continue to inspire us and make us sure that our best years lie ahead.

The flaws in this book are of course our own, and any strengths a large part thanks to the generosity of those who have helped shaped the thinking. Finally, we thank our literary agent, Doe Coover, publisher Peter Neill, book cover designers Laura Bowling and Samira Kordestani, copy editor Jane Crosen, book designer Karen Davidson, managing director World Ocean Observatory Trisha Badger, researcher Elizabeth Stephenson, as well as our ever-present, ever-willing editor, researcher, friend, James Pryor.

Bibliography

Barnosky, Anthony D., et al. (2011). 'Has the Earth's sixth mass extinction already arrived?' *Nature* 471.7336: 51–57.

Barnosky, Anthony D., et al. (2012). 'Approaching a state shift in Earth/'s biosphere'. *Nature* 486.7401: 52–58.

Beston, H. 1928. *The Outermost House*. New York: Doubleday, Doran and Co.

Chambers, Elizabeth G., Mark Fouldon, Helen Handfield-Jones, Steven M. Hankin, and Edward G. Michaels III (1998). *The War for Talent*, McKinsey Quarterly from https://www.mckinseyquarterly.com/The_war_for_talent_3

Cousteau, Jacques-Yves, with Frédéric Dumas (1953). *The Silent World: A Story of Undersea Discovery and Adventure*. Harper and Brothers.

Cullis-Suzuki, S., and D. Pauly. 'Failing the high seas: A global evaluation of regional fisheries management organizations'. Marine Policy (2010), doi:10.1016/j.marpol.2010.03.002

Devaney, Patricia Lee. 'Regional Fisheries Management Organizations: Bringing Order to Disorder', http://www.pon.org/downloads/ien14_4Devaney, accessed 27 October, 2013.

Domingos, Pedro (2015). *The Master Algorithm: How machine learning is reshaping how we live*. pp. 246–7.

Eriksen M, Lebreton LCM, Carson HS, Thiel M, Moore CJ, et al. '*Plastic Pollution in the World's Oceans: More than 5 Trillion Plastic Pieces Weighing over 250,000 Tons Afloat at Sea*'. PLOS ONE. 9 (12): e111913, 10 December, 2014.

Friedman, Thomas L. (2016). *Thank You for Being Late: An Optimist's Guide to Thriving in the Age of Accelerations*. Farrar, Straus and Giroux.

Fukuyama, Francis (1992). *The End of History and the Last Man*. New York: Free Press.

Fuller, R. Buckminster (1969). *Operating Manual Spaceship Earth*. Zurich, Switzerland: Lars Muller Publishers.

Golden, C.D., E.H. Allison, W.W.L. Cheung, M.M. Dey, B.S. Halpern, D.J. McCauley, M. Smith, B.Vaitla, D. Zeller, and S.S. Myers. (2016). 'Nutrition: Fall in fish catch threatens human health.' *Nature* 534: 317–320.

Greenberg, Paul (2011). *Four Fish: The Future of the Last Wild Food*. Penguin Books.

Gulland, J. (1988). *The End of Whaling*. New Scientist. 29 October, 1988. No. 1636. pp. 42–47.

Halpern, B.S., et al. (2012). 'An index to assess the health and benefits of the global ocean'. *Nature* 488:615–620.

Hardin, G. (1968). 'The Tragedy of the Commons.' *Science* 162 (3859): 1243–1248.

Harvey, C. (2017, March 13). 'Carbon dioxide in the atmosphere is rising at the fastest rate ever recorded.' *The Washington Post*.

Häyhä, T., P.L. Lucas, D.P. van Vuuren, S.W. Cornell, and H. Hoff (2016). 'From planetary boundaries to national fair shares of the global safe operating space—How can the scales be bridged?' *Global Environmental Change* 40: 60–72.

Hughes, Terry P., et al. (2017). 'Global warming and recurrent mass bleaching of corals'. *Nature* 543.7645: 373–377.

Ismail, Salim (2014). *Exponential Organizations: Why new organizations are ten times better, faster, and cheaper than yours (and what to do about it)*. Diversion Books.

Kelly, Kevin (2016). *The Inevitable: Understanding the 12 Technological Forces That Will Shape Our Future*. Viking Press.

Kotter, J. P. (1996). *Leading Change*. Boston: Harvard Business School Press.

Kotter, J. P. (1999). *John Kotter on What Leaders Really Do*. Boston: Harvard Business School Press.

Kurlansky, Mark (1997). *Cod: A Biography of the Fish that Changed the World*. Penguin Books.

Kurzweil, Ray (2000). *The Age of Spiritual Machines*. Penguin Putnam.

Manyika, James; Chui, Michael; Miremadi, Mehdi; Bughin, Jacques; George, Katy; Willmott, Paul; Martin (Jan 2017). *Dewhurst Harnessing automation for a future that works*: Report—McKinsey Global Institute

McAfee, Andrew and Brynjolfsson, Erik (2014). *The Second Machine Age: Work, Progress, and Prosperity in a Time of Brilliant Technologies*. W. W. Norton and Company.

McCauley, D.J., M.L. Pinsky, S.R. Palumbi, J.A. Estes, F.H. Joyce, and R.R. Warner (2015). 'Marine defaunation: animal loss in the global oceans'. *Science* 347: 1255641.

McCauley, D.J., P. Woods, B. Sullivan, B. Bergman, C. Jablonicky, A. Roan, M. Hirshfield, K. Boerder, and B. Worm (2016). 'Ending hide and seek at sea'. *Science* 351:1149–1150.

Meadows, D.H., D.L. Meadows, J. Randers, and W.W. Behrens III (1972). *The Limits to Growth*. New York: Universe Books.

Meadows, D.H., D.L. Meadows, and J. Randers (2004). *Limits to Growth: The 30-Year Update*. White River Junction, VT: Chelsea Green Publishing Company.

Meadows, D.H., ed. Diana Wright (2008). *Thinking in Systems: A Primer*. White River Junction, VT: Chelsea Green Publishing Company.

Melville, H. (1851). *Moby-Dick*; or *The Whale*. Harper and Brothers.

Menard, H.W. (1983). *The Ocean of Truth: A Personal History of Global Tectonics*. Princeton Legacy Library. Princeton University Press, July, 2014.

Muoio, D. '19 companies racing to put self-driving cars on the road'. *Business Insider*, 17 October, 2016: http://uk.businessinsider.com/companies-making-driverless-cars-by-2020-2016-10?r=US&IR=T

Myers, R.A., and B. Worm (2003). 'Rapid worldwide depletion of predatory fish communities'. *Nature* 423: 280–283.

Neufeld, L., et al. (2016). *The new plastics economy: rethinking the future of plastics*. World Economic Forum. www.weforum.org/reports/the-new-plastics-economy-rethinking-the-future-of-plastics

Ohmae, Kenichi (1995). *The End of the Nation-State: the Rise of Regional Economies*. New York: Simon and Schuster, Inc.

Paine, Lincoln (2013). *The Sea and Civilization: A Maritime History of the World*. Knopf.

Papworth, S.K., J. Rist, L. Coad, and E.J. Milner-Gulland (2008). 'Evidence for shifting baseline syndrome in conservation'. *Conservation Letters* 2(2):93–100.

Pauly, Daniel (1995). 'Anecdotes and the shifting baseline syndrome of fisheries'. *Trends in Ecology and Evolution* 10(10):430.

Pye, Michael (2015). *The Edge of the World: A Cultural History of the North Sea and the Transformation of Europe*. Pegasus Books.

Ramo, Joshua Cooper (2016). *The Seventh Sense: Power, Fortune, and Survival in the Age of Networks*. Little Brown and Company.

Rifkin, Jeremy (2015). *The Zero Marginal Cost Society: The Internet of Things, the Collaborative Commons, and the Eclipse of Capitalism*. New York: St. Martin's Press. Palgrave MacMillan.

Rockström, J., M. Klum (2015). *Big World, Small Planet: Abundance within Planetary Boundaries*. Stockholm: Bokförlaget Max Ström.

Rockström, J., W. Steffen, K. Noone, Å. Persson, F. S. Chapin, III, E. Lambin, T. M. Lenton, M. Scheffer, C. Folke, H. Schellnhuber, B. Nykvist, C. A. De Wit, T. Hughes, S. van der Leeuw, H. Rodhe, S. Sörlin, P. K. Snyder, R. Costanza, U. Svedin, M. Falkenmark, L. Karlberg, R. W. Corell, V. J. Fabry, J. Hansen, B. Walker, D. Liverman, K. Richardson, P. Crutzen, and J. Foley (2009). 'Planetary boundaries: Exploring the safe operating space for humanity'. Ecology and Society 14(2): 32. www.ecologyandsociety.org/vol14/iss2/art32/.

Ross, Alex (2016). *The Industries of the Future*. New York: Simon & Schuster.

Sachs, Jeffrey (2008). *Common Wealth: Economics for a Crowded Planet*. New York: Penguin Press.

Schmidtko, Sunke, Lothar Stramma, and Martin Visbeck (2017). 'Decline in global oceanic oxygen content during the past five decades'. *Nature* 542.7641: 335–339.

Schwab, Klaus (2017). *The Fourth Industrial Revolution*. Crown Business.

Winchester, Simon (2016). *Pacific*. London, UK: Harper Collins Publishers.

Worm, Boris, et al. (2006). 'Impacts of biodiversity loss on ocean ecosystem services'. *Science* 314.5800: 787–790.

Authors

DR. GREGORY S. STONE is an ocean scientist and explorer with over 10,000 dives using submarines, SCUBA gear, underwater habitats, and robotics. Greg works to find ways for humanity and the ocean to co-exist and support each other in the modern world. He was part of the genesis of the Ocean Health Index and works on marine protected areas, sustainable fishing, aquaculture, climate adaptation, and deep seamount ecology. He's given TED and Davos talks, been featured in documentaries for Discovery and National Geographic. He's authored hundreds of publicatiaons including for *Nature*, *National Geographic*, and three previous books, one a National Outdoor Book Award winner. His numerous accolades and professional associations include the Explorers Club, Pew Fellowship for Marine Conservation, the order of Kiribati Medal, the U.S. National Science Foundation/Navy Antarctic Service medal for Antarctic research, and the top diving award, a NOGI, from National Academy of Underwater Arts and Sciences. He was the science advisor to the atoll nation of Kiribati for the historic UN Paris climate agreement. Greg is Executive Vice President and Chief Scientist for Oceans at Conservation International, and is on the boards of Pacific Rising, The Phoenix Islands Protected Area, and Aqua-Spark. He has degrees in Marine Science (PhD), Marine Policy (MMA), and Human Ecology (BA).

NISHAN DEGNARAIN is a development economist in both the public and  private sectors. Since 2013, he has co-chaired the WEF's Global Agenda Council on Oceans, a group of leading ocean experts from around the world. In recent years, Nishan has been working with the world's leading technology firms in the fields of big data, artificial intelligence, satellite technologies, autonomous vehicles, bio-technology and fin-tech to address some of the world's most pressing challenges.

He is regularly consulted by governments and companies around the world on new models of economic growth, particularly in emerging markets. He sits on several boards, including the China Council's CCICED, and was appointed by the Cabinet of Mauritius to both the Monetary Policy Committee of the Central Bank of Mauritius and the newly created National Ocean Council. He previously worked at the leading consulting firm McKinsey and Company and the UK Prime Minister's Office, beginning his career at the BBC. Nishan is a regular writer and speaker at various international summits such as Davos, and frequently works with leading global governance organisations such as the United Nations, International Seabed Authority, the Global Environment Facility and the World Bank.

Nishan holds undergraduate degrees in Economics and Geography from the University of Cambridge and a postgraduate degree in International Development from Harvard University's Kennedy School of Government. He was recognised as a Young Global Leader by the World Economic Forum.